*The Arms of the Borough of Penzance.*

# A HISTORY OF CORNWALL

THE DARWEN COUNTY HISTORY SERIES

# A History of Cornwall

## IAN SOULSBY

*Drawings by* Michelle Richards

*Cartography by* Ian Soulsby

PHILLIMORE

1986

Published by
PHILLIMORE & CO. LTD.
Shopwyke Hall, Chichester, Sussex

ISBN 0 85033 612 0

*Typeset in the United Kingdom by:*
*Fidelity Processes - Selsey - Sussex*

Printed and bound in Great Britain by
Biddles Ltd, Guildford and King's Lynn

# Contents

# List of Plates

The author wishes to thank the following for permission to reproduce photographs: R. E. Gibson, Scilly Isles, plate 32; *Glasney Press*, Falmouth, plates 16, 18, 23, 24, 25, 26, 29, 30, 31, 33, 34, 37, 39, 40, 41, 42, 43 and 44; Western Morning News Co. Ltd., Plymouth, plates 11, 12, 13, 38, 45, 46, 47 and 48; Woodmansterne Publications Ltd., plates 21 (photo: Howard Moore), 22 (photo: Malcolm Osman) and 35 (photo: Jeremy Marks).

# List of Maps

# List of Text Illustrations

# Acknowledgements

My interest in history was first stimulated as a schoolboy in West Cornwall and I shall always be grateful to my former teachers, Maurice Hogg and Tom Pascoe, for their expertise and encouragement. I also owe a very special debt to Professor Henry Loyn whose sheer enthusiasm and ability to stimulate others can only be appreciated by those who have had the privilege to study under him. When I was an undergraduate at University College Cardiff and later as a research student, he was responsible for directing my energies towards early medieval Cornwall and has always been willing to lend an ear ever since. I owe him a great debt of gratitude as I do Professor A. O. H. Jarman and Morfydd Owen who generously allowed me to inflict my opinions on their undergraduates and to conduct a series of extra-mural lectures on Cornwall and Brittany. Without the confidence which those experiences provided, this book would never have been attempted.

My most obvious debt is to the countless scholars whose specialist work provides the backbone of this study. Any general county history which embraces such a lengthy time-span must inevitably be a work of synthesis and without the labour of others this book would not have been possible. I would specifically like to thank Dave Evans for his help with the changing interpretations of prehistory and Oliver Padel for commenting on a draft of Chapter Nine. The Cornwall Committee for Rescue Archaeology generously provided me with information on several of the more obscure sites while Brian Baker has given tremendous assistance with the photographs. It is also a pleasure to thank Michelle Richards for her fine line illustrations which are a charming supplement to the text. Finally I would like to express my gratitude to my mother for her valuable support and to Anna for her companionship and help with the index.

# Introduction

Cornwall is England's most south-westerly county; as a geographical entity, it is almost instantly recognisable by its contours. With the longest coastline in the country (some 326 miles), it is bounded by the sea for more than 80 per cent of its perimeter and virtually detached from the rest of Britain by the River Tamar. Although now one of the most visited parts of England, for much of its history Cornwall remained beyond the mainstream of national life, its character rooted in a Celtic past and its own language, commonly spoken until its rapid decline in the 17th and 18th centuries. To Tudor antiquarians, this was the land of 'West Wales', while to an Italian commentator, Giovanni Botero, it was also something special, the 'fourth part of greate Britaine . . . because of the dissimilitude of the language unto other parts'. I have tried wherever possible to place Cornwall's history within this Celtic orbit, not because it has become fashionable but because I believe the approach to be justified in its own right.

With such a special identity it is not surprising that Cornwall's past has attracted a great deal of scholarly attention. Archaeologists have been particularly active in recent years and their work has caused many traditional interpretations to be revised, if not abandoned altogether. Prehistory, language and dialect, the Middle Ages, Tudor Cornwall, the Civil War and the Industrial Revolution have all attracted their specialists, but there has been no modern county history available to the general reader for many years. Like others in this series, this book attempts to fill that vacuum by providing a readable account which at the same time incorporates the findings of the most recent research. Whether it is possible in a book as selective as this to satisfy everyone is, of course, another matter. That verdict rests with those who read it, as it always must.

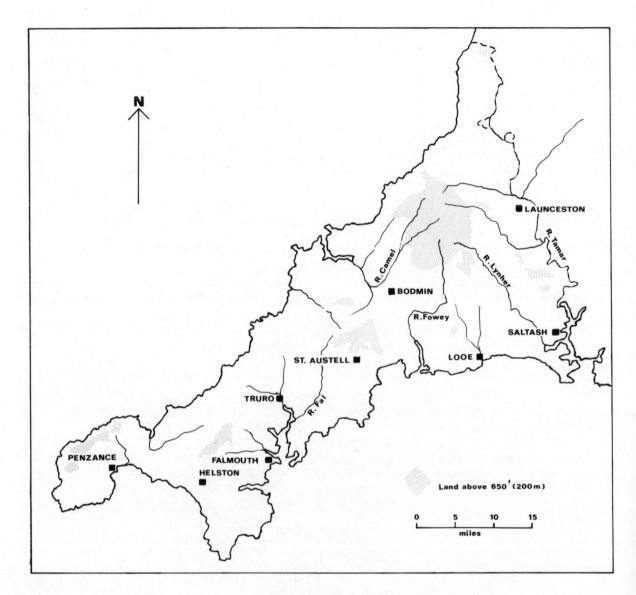

Relief map of Cornwall.

# I Prehistoric Cornwall

About 13,000 years ago, when the last ice age was in full retreat and Britain was still joined to mainland Europe, the peninsula which we now know as Cornwall would have been one of the most inhospitable regions of the western world. A severe climate, near-arctic conditions and a landscape resembling a polar desert would have made vegetation growth impossible, and another 3,000 years had to pass before the gradual rise in temperature allowed the slow advance of first scrubland and then forest. It was at this time, during the Palaeolithic period, that the first inhabitants began to arrive, although we know very little about these very early pioneers in Cornwall. Indeed, the pattern of human activity only begins to clear after about 7000 B.C., when we can envisage a Mesolithic population of hunter-gatherers moving from place to place in search of migratory animals like red deer and wild pigs and in spring and autumn exploiting the resources of the sea as shellfish and whitefish made their seasonal incursions into coastal waters. At Trevose Head, on the north coast, archaeologists have identified one of the county's most important and productive Mesolithic sites which yielded evidence of perhaps 6,000 years of prehistoric activity. Over 800 flints were recorded and the scale and variety of the finds reminds us that they were put to a multitude of uses, scrapers for skin and hides, weapons for hunting, and tools for collecting and breaking open limpets, mussels and other varieties of shellfish. With fruit and berries also forming an integral part of their diet, these early inhabitants had clearly proved adept at exploiting the diversity of the natural resources available to them.

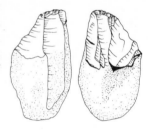

*Mesolithic flints*

During the fourth millennium B.C. this Mesolithic lifestyle was transformed by the infusion not only of new technologies but of new blood as fresh colonists moved westwards from southern Britain, bringing with them a knowledge of pottery manufacture and, more importantly, agriculture. This progression into what is termed the Neolithic period was characterised by the introduction of both arable farming and animal husbandry, practices which gave rise to the funda-mental innovation of permanent settlements. Several archaeological sites have provided evidence of Neolithic activity in Cornwall, like Poldowrian on the Lizard and Bodwen near Lostwithiel, but Carn Brea near Redruth has recently proved to be the most revealing. Here a two-acre hill-top enclosure, part of a settlement pattern which had been established throughout northern and western Europe, was found to

13

contain a number of timber huts while on the southern slopes beyond the defences indications were also found of field clearances and cereal cultivation. Detailed examination also produced evidence of long-distance trade while a hint, perhaps, of the tensions of Neolithic society was provided by the discovery of an unusually large number of arrowheads, which suggests that the community was periodically called upon to defend itself against the attacks of unfriendly neighbours.

With the advent of permanent settlements came another development, the construction of monuments which today are mainly to be found in moorland areas where they have been able to escape from the conse-quences of later agricultural clearances. Among the most distinctive features are the Penwith chamber tombs, a type series found all over Cornwall but named after the area in which they were first recognised. These structures, which seem to have been much more than mere burial mounds, probably fulfilled a number of ceremonial and territorial rôles. While they vary in form, the basic model consists of mighty upright slabs, or orthostats, capped with a large, flattish stone, although archaeologists no longer accept the previously held view that they were originally covered with an earthen mound which was subsequently eroded by the elements. Fine examples of these monuments, variously known as quoits, cromlechs and dolmens, can be seen at Zennor, Chun and Lanyon in the far west of the county. About another dozen quoits have been identified elsewhere but the fate of the Devil's Coyt (a dialect spelling form) near St Columb Major, enterprisingly used as a pigsty until it collapsed in the 1840's and then as a source of hedging stone, reminds us that they were probably much more numerous, like countless other types of early Cornish monuments.

The chamber tombs and the immense human effort required to erect them suggest that society was developing an important degree of organisation and cohesion. This increased stability also seems to have contributed to a growth in population and even possibly to a certain amount of land pressure as the unsophisticated methods of land utilisation were no longer capable of supporting the growing numbers. In west Cornwall, at least, this development may well have become pronounced by the end of the Neolithic and Professor Charles Thomas, in his recent study of the Isles of Scilly, has advanced the view that this factor lay behind a planned colonisation of the islands by land-hungry emigrants from the Penwith peninsula.

During the early part of the second millennium, c. 1800 B.C., Cornwall was host to a new group of settlers known as the Beaker folk who were associated with a distinctive style of reddish-brown decorated pottery and greater variety of burial practices. The Beaker homeland lay on the continent, although in Cornwall's case they may have arrived indirectly via Wales and Ireland, bringing with them a specialist know-ledge of mineral working. They smelted copper for axe heads and matched it with tin to produce a superior alloy, bronze, and archaeologists interpret the arrival of this new technology as signalling another era

*Neolithic beaker
from Trevedra,
St Just*

14

in prehistory, the Bronze Age. Weapons, tools, pottery and other implements became more sophisticated while burial rituals were more diverse. Barrows of earth and stone were favoured and these survive in large numbers on upland areas like Bodmin Moor and St Breock Downs, along with stone cists in which cremated bones and various grave-goods were deposited. An excavated cist at Gunwalloe on the Lizard yielded three pots of human ashes as well as the unburnt bones of a young rabbit, a toad and three birds.

A major problem with the Bronze Age in Cornwall, and as we have seen it is one shared with earlier periods, is that many sites have been destroyed by centuries of agricultural and mining activity. During the past 20 years, however, several key excavations have made important contributions to our understanding of this period. At Trevisker, near St Eval, detailed examination identified a community which lived in circular wooden huts, kept livestock like the horned oxen and also engaged in some arable cultivation. At Stannon Down, St Breward, a hut circle settlement has been excavated and along with it an associated system of rectilinear and curvilinear fields, while at Gwithian near Hayle the community worked small, square fields which were hardly much bigger than modern allotments. All this points to a great increase in farming throughout Cornwall and to a settled society working its permanent fields and fixed grazing areas. Important trading links had been established with other coastal regions like Brittany, Wales and Ireland, and this led to the gradual acquisition of more ornate goods and implements such as the bronze rapier dredged from the River Fowey, the nine gold bracelets unearthed from a field boundary at Amalveor near Towednack, and the very rare bronze saw which was discovered at St Mawgan on the north coast.

*Bronze Age spearhead from Tredarvah*

This stability also seems to have been a key factor behind an increase in megalithic or monument-building activity which was primarily directed towards the construction of stone circles, a practice which had its roots in the Neolithic but accelerated during the early Bronze Age. There are nearly thirty of these stone circles in Cornwall with the greatest concentration on Bodmin Moor and in the far west. Some four miles north of Liskeard stand the Hurlers, three adjacent circles lying on a N.N.E.–S.S.W. axis, while in the west the better known examples include Boskednan, Tregeseal, Boscawen Un and, above all, the Merry Maidens near Lamorna. Even the most cursory glance at any of these monuments would be enough to remind us of the vast amount of human effort which must have gone into their construction, so much in fact that many theories, some pure fantasy, others quite logical, have been advanced as to their original function and significance. An earlier generation of antiquaries, like the 18th-century Cornishman William Borlase, linked them with mysterious, druidical ceremonies and conjured up images of eerie rituals and sacrifices. Others have linked them with astronomy, pointing out that many are often aligned with other circles as well as with the sun at solstices, and accordingly

*Bant's Carn: a Scillonian entrance grave*

have accredited their builders with a sophisticated knowledge of mathematics, of measurements like the 'megalithic yard' and an understanding of the movement of the planets. Modern authorities, however, like Aubrey Burl and John Barnatt are more sceptical and take the reasonable view that these circles were essentially meeting places, focal points for ritual, worship and perhaps even economic activities. Several other types of Bronze Age monument forms can also be found in Cornwall, although providing a satisfactory explanation of their original function is another matter. Standing stones, or menhirs, which are again concentrated in Penwith where some bear curious musical names like 'the Pipers' and the 'Blind Fiddler', remain difficult to interpret, although another group, the Entrance Graves or chambered cairns of Penwith and Scilly, are now seen as structures associated as much with ritual and fertility as with burial. Indeed, the more archaeological knowledge advances, the more we are inclined to envisage all early monuments as having fulfilled not one but a variety of territorial and spiritual functions.

By the end of the Bronze Age, *c*. 800 B.C., there are indications that the climate was deteriorating, and certainly the soil conditions on the higher moorland areas were causing concern with the spread of peat. In Cornwall this trend brought about changes in the distribution of population as Bodmin Moor and similar upland zones were gradually abandoned in favour of the warmer and more fertile lowlands. This process was contemporary with major advances in metal working as knowledge of iron manufacture was spreading throughout Britain. The first indications of iron working came from the Black Sea region and particularly from the province of Anatolia in modern Turkey. The new technology swept across a Europe which was in the throes of tribal conflict and large scale migrations, and of these restless peoples the most important from the Cornish standpoint were the Celts. The Celts were a warrior society initially distinguished by their habit of burying their dead in urns in level cemeteries and from *c*. 1200 B.C. they had begun to spread westwards from their homelands in eastern Europe. At Hallstatt in Austria archaeologists have carried out extensive excavations of a large cemetery and substantial salt workings, the use of a salt as a preservative being a practice particularly associated with the Celts. As these people became more sophisticated a more developed social order was established and by 500 B.C. their economic and spiritual worlds had become quite complex. The La Tène Celts, as these later tribes are known after an important site in Switzerland, were technologically advanced, skilled workers in metal and wood, and efficient traders with their Greek and Roman contemporaries.

Britain, meanwhile, was developing her own Celtic culture as increasing contact with the continent brought new influences, and running parallel with this marked increase in trade was a long period of piecemeal Celtic colonisation which began in the seventh century and which then accelerated in the first century B.C. The newcomers were gradually

16

1. Menhir, or standing stone, on Boswens Common.

2. Holed stone on the bleak upland of Carn Kenidjack, scene of considerable prehistoric activity.

3. St Piran's cross in the churchyard at Perranzabuloe.

4. Ornamental Celtic cross bearing the figure of Christ, St Buryan
churchyard.

5. The collegiate church of St Endellion, Port Isaac.

6. Repositioned churchyard cross in Ludgvan,
near Penzance, overlooking the village square
and public house.

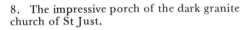

DHE COF A
MYGHAL JOSEP
AN GOF
HA
THOMAS FLAMANK
HEMBRYNKYSY AN LU KERNEWEK
A GESKERDHAS BYS DHE LOUNDRES
HA CODHEVEL ENA DYALANS
METHEVEN 1497
"Y A'S TEVYTH HANOW A
BES VYNYTHA HA BRY A DHUR
HEP MERWEL"
DREHEVYS GANS MEBYON KERNOW.
1966

IN MEMORY OF
MICHAEL JOSEPH
THE SMITH
AND
THOMAS FLAMANK
LEADERS OF THE CORNISH HOST
WHO MARCHED TO LONDON
AND SUFFERED VENGEANCE THERE
JUNE 1497
"THEY SHALL HAVE A NAME
PERPETUAL AND A FAME PERMANENT
AND IMMORTAL"
ERECTED BY MEBYON KERNOW.
1966

7.  Bilingual memorial to the leaders of the 1497 rebellion, St Keverne.

8.  The impressive porch of the dark granite church of St Just.

9.  An early print of Launceston Gate. The room at the top was used as the town gaol.

10.  Farming landscape of West Penwith.

11.  Launceston Castle.

12.  Restormel Castle.

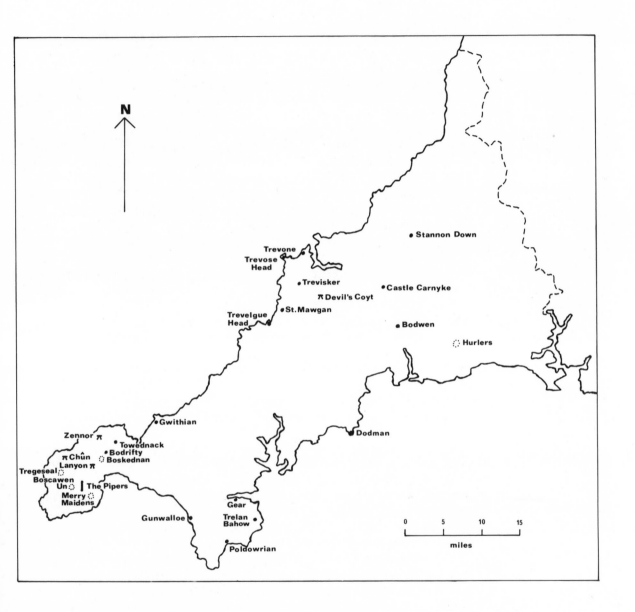

Prehistoric Cornwall, showing sites mentioned in the text.

17

assimilated into the native Bronze Age population and from this fusion emerged a number of dialects from which the Cornish language is ultimately descended. In Cornwall evidence from this period is fairly substantial and over 600 Iron Age sites have been identified, many by aerial photography and the analysis of crop marks. It is clear that the typical settlement was the Round, a circular or sub-circular enclosure defended by a single bank and ditch and containing stone or wooden round houses and outbuildings. Beyond these defended farms lay the fields, now completely obliterated in lowland areas where they are recognisable only by cropmarks of ditches. In Penwith, as at Bodrifty near Penzance, the associated fields remain as stony banks or field walls which are maintained to the present day. Among the most recent examples to have been excavated was the smaller Threemilestone Round near Truro where an area of *c.* 3,000 square yards was enclosed by a 10-ft. bank and ditch with two further smaller ditches beyond. In west Cornwall, again, another settlement model was the 'courtyard house', a form which has a counterpart in north-east Wales with the 'enclosed homesteads' of Gwynedd.

At Chysauster, a village of at least ten courtyard houses, a typical house had a central courtyard surrounded by dwellings and storerooms set within a formidable stone wall. The courtyard house village at Carn Euny, also in Penwith, contained three main houses which have been excavated and the site appears to have been occupied for at least 700 years during the early Iron Age and Roman periods. These communities, and many others like them, established their associated field systems, clearing away surface stone to make small permanent fields enclosed by dry stone hedges. Sadly, much of the Chysauster field system has been recently bulldozed to meet the needs of modern farming, but on the uplands around Zennor it is still possible to look down on a remarkably well preserved Iron Age agricultural landscape. Of burial sites, Harlyn Bay is the most important. Excavation of this cemetery between 1900–5 revealed 130 slate-lined graves or cists some 15 ft. below the sand surface, and some of them contained Iberian brooches which indicate trading links with Spain. Another burial site was located at Trevone, while at Trelan Bahow near St Keverne a grave of an obviously important female was found to contain some, at least, of her worldly possessions including rings, bracelets, brooches, a necklace and a bronze mirror.

The Iron Age communities were also great builders of hillforts and many of these defended structures can be found throughout Cornwall. One of the most impressive examples is Castle-an-Dinas, situated in the upland area mid-way between Penzance and St Ives and less than a mile from the settlement at Chysauster. With an overall diameter of 436 ft. (133 m), this hillfort had four lines of defence while recent surveying of the surrounding slopes revealed evidence of a complex patchwork of small, irregular fields worked by the inhabitants. At Chun Castle in Penwith the ramparts were said to have been 15 ft. high until they were robbed during the 1840's to provide stone for the construction of the new north pier at Penzance. Other substantial hillforts include Castle Canyke near Bodmin and Gear on the southern side of the Helford River. In addition to hillforts, over twenty cliff castles have been identified around the coastal promontories of the county. These were fortified headlands defended across the 'neck' by one or more ramparts, and appear to have fulfilled a variety of economic, defensive and settlement functions. Fine examples include Trevelgue Head near Newquay, the Dodman near St Austell and Chun Castle east of Porthcurno which also sports the famous 'Logan Rock' perched on top of a rocky outcrop within the fort. Another feature associated with the Iron Age in Cornwall were the *fogous*, a term derived from the Cornish word *fogo* meaning a cave. These structures have their equivalents in Brittany, S.W. Scotland and Ireland and amount to underground passageways roofed with large granite slabs. While they are to be found as an integral part of small settlements their original function is unclear and suggestions have ranged from storage chambers, places of retreat during times of attack, or perhaps they were linked with worship and spiritual matters.

*A 'fogou' from Pendeen*

As Cornwall entered the first millennium A.D. it is quite evident that the regional economy had become much more developed and diverse. Farming, fishing, pottery manufacture, salt and metal working all played their part while tin, particularly, had already become the subject of a flourishing trade with the Mediterranean world. Other important maritime connections had been established with Ireland, Wales and Brittany, regions which were to make an increasingly important contribution throughout and well beyond the approaching centuries of Roman authority.

*Lanyon Quoit*

19

# II Romans, Celts and Saxons

Julius Caesar had first launched an exploratory expedition to Britain in 55 B.C. but this had been a brief campaign restricted to the south-east and a full-scale Roman invasion was not attempted until A.D. 43 when Emperor Claudius ordered a large force across the Channel from Boulogne. These invaders, however, like the Normans after them, were to find the task of subduing the natives a long and costly affair, and over a decade passed before the first Roman legions penetrated the south-west. In A.D. 55–60 a legionary fortress was built at Exeter and, as the Second Augustan legion gradually progressed westwards, a chain of garrisoned forts was also erected although only one Cornish example, Nanstallon on the River Camel, has been identified. This solitary site, in fact, reflects the paucity of our knowledge of the military subjection of Cornwall, and the material cultural contacts with the Romans are restricted to a solitary villa near Camborne and a few milestones. It is accepted that a military conquest had been completed by A.D. 61, but 14 years later the legion at Exeter was withdrawn and the peninsula settled down to four centuries of only nominal Roman rule. While there was undoubtedly a steady diffusion of Roman culture, laws and language there was no Roman town west of Exeter, and the bulk of the population can hardly have been greatly disturbed by their new overlords, perhaps making contact only with visiting tax collectors and the occasional trading party in the market for tin. Quite a few coin hoards are known, however, together with many more instances of individual coin finds and this suggests the adoption, in part at least, of a money-based economy along Roman lines.

*Late Iron Age coin*
*from Carn Brea*

Throughout the Roman period the population of Cornwall continued to live in the scattered 'rounds' and 'courtyard houses' favoured by their Iron Age predecessors. These, for the most part, were heavily defended like the first-century 'round' at Castle Gotha, St Austell, while excavation of similar sites at Carlidnack near Mawnan and Shortlanesend near Truro have confirmed the continuing popularity of this settlement model. In the far west the density of 'rounds' seems to have been as high as one per square mile, although the continued need to live within such defended enclosures must tell us something about the unsettled nature of society at this time. Hillforts, on the other hand, do not seem to have continued in use as they did in Wales, and if we regard these as having been the main centres of a developing social order, the seats of local rulers, then the Romans evidently had control over tribal hierarchies.

20

For the inhabitants, economic life continued very much as before. Inevitably agriculture remained paramount with the emphasis on live-stock while industry was largely confined to pottery manufacture and a few salt workings. While trade links with Brittany continued, the demand for Cornish tin declined as the Romans exploited more accessible reserves in Spain. Diodurus Siculus, citing the account of the Greek traveller Pytheas, *c.* 325 B.C., had noted that 'in Britain the inhabitants of a promontory called Belerion [Land's End] ... prepare the tin ... they beat the metal into masses shaped like an ox hide and carry it to a certain island lying off Britain called Ictis' (probably St Michael's Mount). If this trade had fallen off during the early phase of Roman occupation, it seems to have revived in the mid-third century and by the end of the fourth Cornish tin was again in demand throughout the civilised world.

*Roman pottery lamp from St Ives*

If Roman authority in Cornwall was essentially nominal, the four centuries of incorporation within the Empire nevertheless precipitated a number of important social and political developments. In A.D. 80 the new Roman governor Agricola initiated a process of administrative reorganisation by which each recognisable tribal unit became a self-governing region or *civitas*. In the south-west the regional capital was fixed at Exeter, then *Isca Dumnoniorum*, a name which provides a pointer to the developing identity of the whole peninsula. To the Romans the inhabitants of Cornwall, Devon and west Somerset were the *Dumnonii*, the descendants of the Iron Age Celtic settlers who had absorbed the older Bronze Age population. While the Dumnonii had extensive maritime contacts they had little intercourse with the Belgic tribes of south and east England. They spoke, but did not write, a primitive Celtic tongue which was absorbing Latin loan-words and which, by the 10th century, had become sufficiently different from the speech of other regions to be classified as Cornish. It seems likely that within this increasingly civilian-controlled region smaller administrative units or *pagi* came into being, each responsible to the authorities at Exeter but under the control of a local chieftain enjoying a substantial degree of autonomy.

*Roman altar on Tresco, Isles of Scilly*

In 410 Britain ceased to be part of the Roman Empire. Most occupying forces had in fact already been withdrawn to deal with an increasingly rebellious continent, and the authorities in Rome no longer had the resources to satisfy 'the groans of the Britons'. Even before the last legions had embarked, however, the coastal regions of Britain were already attracting Saxon and Goidelic (Irish) settlers and it was becoming clear that the end of one age of occupation was about to be followed by another and equally important one.

Throughout the fifth and sixth centuries East Anglia and south-east England experienced a substantial folk colonisation by Anglo-Saxon farmers in search of new lands. Gradually they spread westwards until even the remote people of Dumnonia were obliged to face up to the reality of these Germanic intruders. Already, however, the people of

21

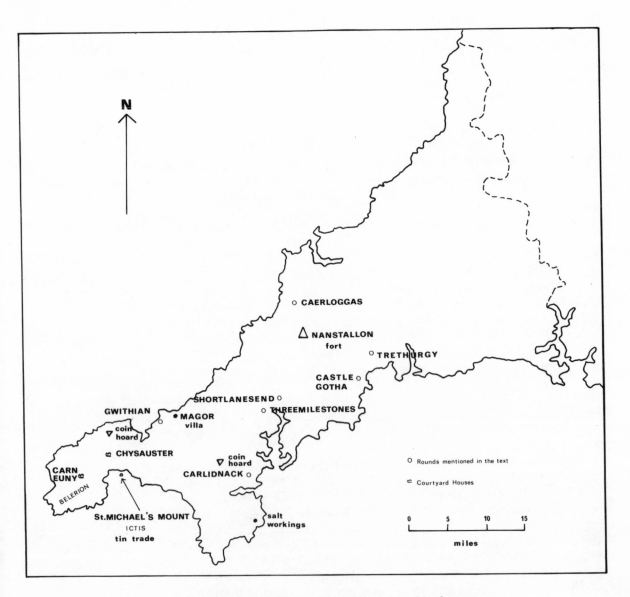

Romano-British Cornwall, showing sites mentioned in the text.

The map contains the following labels:

N

○ CAERLOGGAS

△ NANSTALLON
fort

○ TRETHURGY

CASTLE ○
GOTHA

SHORTLANESEND ○

○ THREEMILESTONES

GWITHIAN

● MAGOR
villa

▽ coin
hoard

CHYSAUSTER

▽ coin
hoard

CARLIDNACK ○

CARN
EUNY

BELERION

St. MICHAEL'S MOUNT

ICTIS
tin trade

● salt
workings

○ Rounds mentioned in the text

Courtyard Houses

0      5      10      15

miles

22

Cornwall were being faced with newcomers from a different direction, Ireland. Since the fifth century Goidelic settlers had been establishing colonies in western Scotland and the extremities of west Wales and from the latter they began to cross the Bristol Channel to Cornwall. Evidence for this migration is derived from several sources, including the rather dubious church dedications and later 'Saint's Lives', but more reliably from the inscribed stones which they left behind. These people possessed a unique form of script known as Ogham whereby letters were represented by a variety of lines cut into the face of standing stones, and in Cornwall there are four of these stones plus another two on the Devon side of the Tamar, all commemorating some local chieftain or dignitary. The distribution of these memorials shows a clear concentration in north-east Cornwall above the Camel estuary, although other standing stones bearing Irish names but with Latin inscriptions can also be found in the west. Whether these should be interpreted as indications of large scale colonisation, however, is far from clear. Such a view was fashionable until relatively recently but is now questioned, and the absence of Irish loan-words in the Cornish vocabulary argues against a substantial Goidelic presence. We may be talking about no more than a few pockets of settlers or a localised aristocratic take-over which led to the dissemination of Irish cultural influences.

If many points remain to be clarified on this issue, uncertainty also surrounds another contemporary development, the colonisation of Armorica (Brittany) by emigrants from Dumnonia and east Wales. This movement of Celtic-speaking peoples across the English Channel has traditionally been interpreted in terms of a flight from the advancing Anglo-Saxons, but more recent writers have concluded that the process began well before their presence was felt in the south-west. The first Dumnonian settlers, in fact, may well have made the crossing in the fourth century, although there was undoubtedly an acceleration in the sixth century which other scholars have seen as a consequence of increased Goidelic activity in Cornwall. Whatever the explanation, the creation of this Celtic-speaking colony on the European mainland proved to add a major dimension to the future history of Cornwall and led to a close relationship for centuries to follow. The 12th-century chronicler Gerald of Wales was able to observe 'that the people of Cornwall and Armorica speak a language almost identical', while medieval Cornish towns were home to many Breton merchants. Fishermen sought refuge in each other's harbours and this cultural intercourse must have been a major factor in prolonging the life of the Cornish language. Even today the Cornish retain an affinity for their Breton cousins, and choirs, folk singers, 'twinned-town' associations as well as a host of other cultural organisations regularly sustain the links first established so many centuries ago.

The references which have been made to inscribed standing stones and chroniclers remind us that the age of recorded history had now begun. The Irish settlers may well have employed their Ogham script, but the overwhelming impact of Roman culture dictated that Latin be the language of formal communication. The legacy of Rome is also evident in the political development of the south-west, which gathered pace throughout the centuries of migration and colonisation. As we have already seen, Dark Age Cornwall was part of the larger Celtic kingdom of Dumnonia which seems originally to have extended as far east as the River Parrett in Somerset but was now steadily contracting in the face of Anglo-Saxon expansion. While no written evidence of the nature of Dumnonian administration has survived, if it ever existed at all, a possible pattern has been gleaned from the study of inscriptions, place-names and later chroniclers, all considered in the light of what is known of other regions. Professor Thomas has envisaged a tribal system of authority which was perhaps based on a continuation of the Roman *pagi* system whereby the whole region was divided into a number of districts or *pagi*, each with its own *regulus* or chieftain. This would be in keeping with the conclusions of Dr. Wendy Davies who has shown that in sixth-century Wales local kings — and the title should not be seen in its medieval context — ruled over small areas of little more than 15-mile radius. Above the petty Dumnonian rulers would have been the regional king and the names of several have survived, including Constantine, born *c*. 500 and described by the chronicler Gildas as 'the tyrannical whelp of the unclean lioness of Damnonia'. This interpretation makes it possible to account for the many notables remembered on inscribed stones and for the known survival of local chieftains well into the Saxon era when the royal house itself had been displaced. In 875, for example, the Welsh *Chronicle of the Princes* records the drowning of 'Dumnarth, king of Cornwall' and his name, in its Old Cornish form *Doniert*, is also inscribed on a cross base near Liskeard. Again, an inscription on the old Penzance market cross to a 'King Ricatus' probably records a local *regulus* who lived during the early 10th century.

*A Celtic chariot*

If this administrative model is essentially an intelligent guess, we are even less confident when it comes to the social structure of pre-medieval Cornwall. No Cornish equivalent of the 'Welsh Laws' is known, although it is difficult to believe that the region was isolated from the common social stratification of Dark Age Europe. Below the tribal and sub-tribal hierarchies hereditary slavery was common, although it was possible to obtain freedom through a process of manumission as the early 10th-century *Bodmin Gospels* reveal. There are indications that settlement patterns were changing with the abandonment of the earlier favoured 'rounds' and the development of agricultural settlements associated with *tre* place-names, many of which later emerged as medieval manorial centres. The substantial element of academic uncertainty which surrounds other aspects of this period, however, has much to do with the imminent collapse of Dumnonia and its institutions and the superimposition of new cultural and administrative models. The kingdom, after all, had been in retreat for centuries as Anglo-Saxon colonists

24

continued to push westwards, until by the eighth century only Cornwall remained to enjoy a brief period of uneasy independence.

The stages in the westward expansion of Wessex have been comprehensively reconstructed by W. G. Hoskins and H. P. R. Finberg and it is only necessary to make a few cosmetic modifications to their accounts. It is important to envisage Anglo-Saxon expansion as a haphazard process which spanned several centuries and not as a series of planned military operations. The exodus to Brittany coupled with the effects of the sporadic outbreaks of plague, which affected most of Europe in the fifth, sixth and seventh centuries, must have resulted in marked depopulation of many areas, and in that light we can envisage a steady Anglo-Saxon movement which occasionally provoked Celtic military resistance followed in turn by a series of reprisals. The process began in 682 when Centwine 'drover the Britons as far as the sea', probably back into the north-eastern corner of Cornwall. After this campaign the frontier was probably the Ottery–Tamar line, but in 710 Ine of Wessex defeated Geraint of Dumnonia and advanced across the Tamar as far as the River Lynher. This success was followed by a royal charter to Glastonbury granting lands between the two rivers and the large number of English place-names in the area reinforces the view that substantial Anglo-Saxon colonisation followed Ine's victory. In 722, however, aided by a force from Wales, the Cornish launched a counter-attack and defeated the Saxons at *Hehil*, an unidentified site but perhaps somewhere along the Camel estuary. This was to provide only a temporary respite, however, and in 753 Cuthred of Wessex launched a new campaign which was continued by his successor Cynewulf. In 815 Egbert is said to have 'harried Cornwall from east to west', probably an exaggeration, but a counter-offensive was launched 10 years later when the Cornish crossed the Tamar and fought the enemy at Galford. A crucial stage was reached in 838 when the Cornish threw in their lot with Viking marauders and advanced against King Egbert, only to be defeated at Hingston Down near Callington. Cornwall was now nominally incorporated into the kingdom of Wessex and the Cornish bishop, Kenstec, was compelled to acknowledge the superiority of the archbishop of Canterbury. A sizeable amount of Cornish land was granted off, but it is significant that most of the estates involved were confined to the northern and eastern areas and for the rest this Saxon 'conquest' seems to have meant very little. As we have already seen, petty rulers continued to exercise power and almost another century had to pass before the whole of Cornwall was assimilated into the newly united kingdom of England. It was Athelstan, 924–39, who completed the process, and he appears to have devoted considerable attention to south-western affairs, dealing with a threatened uprising and holding councils in Devon in 928 and 931, when he seems to have reorganised the six Cornish tribal divisions of *pagi* into hundreds in line with the English pattern. According to the chronicler William of Malmesbury, Athelstan then fixed the Tamar as the county

*King Athelstan*

25

*A 'bar-lug' cooking pot*

boundary, a decision based on geographical convenience rather than racial division, as the Celts were by then clearly in a minority east of the Lynher.

While Cornish political independence had come to an end it is nonetheless important to make a distinction between conquest and settlement. While the eastern districts had been exposed to steady Anglo-Saxon colonisation for some time, the central and western areas had remained relatively untouched. Place-name evidence points to the paucity of colonists west of the Lynher where they were so rare as to be specially distinguished by the Cornish with the suffix *Sawsen* (Saxon or English), as in the case of Nansawsen and Tresawsen. The investigation of settlement patterns, coin distribution, and pottery types has also strengthened this conclusion and it is significant that in a 'land of saints' very few Cornish parishes, perhaps only three, are dedicated to specifically Saxon saints. Life, in short, went on very much as before, and for the inhabitants of, say, the coastal community at Mawgan Porth, whose village was excavated in the 1950s, there can have been no noticeable change. Somebody obviously acquired the silver penny of Aethelred II unearthed by the archaeologists, but the inhabitants continued to eke out a living, make their 'bar-lug' pottery and live in the multi-chambered courtyard houses much as their predecessors had done. Again, while most of the land had passed into Anglo-Saxon hands by the eve of the Norman Conquest, and only one instance is known of a land grant being made by a Cornishman in the 10th century, it seems likely that even the majority of the new landholders lived elsewhere.

As always with the Celts, however, the loss of political independence was only to be followed by the growth of myths and legends and talk of leaders who would rise up to free the people from their new masters. The greatest of these traditions, of course, is that of King Arthur who is always associated with the cliff-top castle at Tintagel. The Arthurian legend was firmly established by the 12th century and taken to fanciful extremes by Geoffrey of Monmouth in his *History of the Kings of Britain* written *c.* 1136. Earlier, in 1113, we hear of a Cornishman who fought with the manservant of a visiting clergyman claiming that Arthur was still alive! Yet the Welsh and Bretons also lay claim to him and, if Arthur did exist, which is quite probable, it is better to envisage him in the rôle of a Celtic resistance leader, fighting the Saxons on a number of fronts, whose exploits reached untold heights in the imagination of medieval chroniclers and Tudor story-tellers.

*A medieval depiction of King Arthur: not a natural seafarer*

For over a century after Athelstan's reign Cornwall enjoyed a respite from the turmoil which had characterised the preceding two hundred years. English authority was now unchallenged, and the absorption of cultural and linguistic influences proceeded in a peaceful and subconscious fashion. At the end of the 10th century, however, this scene was briefly disturbed by outside aggressors when a handful of Cornwall's villages and churches were the target of Viking raiders.

26

Simeon of Durham recorded an attack in 981 which destroyed the monastery at Padstow while in 997 a 'host of Danes . . . ravaged Cornwall . . . thence returning around *Penwithsteort* [Land's End], and going up the mouth of the River Tamar they landed, and without opposition continued their burning and renewed their slaughter'. Fortunately this was to be only a temporary disturbance and, compared with other maritime regions of western Britain, Cornwall was not again to be exposed to 'the fury of the Northmen'. Viking manpower, after all, had its limits and this was hardly a county of riches to warrant regular expeditions. Cornwall's poverty, in fact, was soon to be confirmed with the arrival of the Normans who were about to open another chapter in the history of Britain.

# III A Land of Saints: The Early Cornish Church

The earliest Celts were a pagan people for whom religion and super-stition were inseparable. They worshipped numerous underground gods and attributed special mysterious significance to physical features such as woods, springs, wells and pools. They were great practitioners of cults, the head being particularly revered and commonly carved in wood and stone. Classical writers wrote of the existence of Druids although frequently associating them with mystery and human sacrifice in a deliberate attempt to depict the Celts as undesirable barbarians in desperate need of the civilising influence of Mediterranean culture. In reality, as Julius Caesar himself observed, these Druids do not seem to have been priests but a kind of official class, well versed in tradition and learning, who acted in the manner of ceremonial supervisors.

Unfortunately we know virtually nothing about the specific pagan practices of the early Dumnonii. Celtic religion was essentially an open-air activity which probably utilised existing stone monuments and circles leaving little tangible evidence behind. Most of our knowledge of Celtic paganism comes from Ireland, which was untouched by the Romans, or from Gaul which was close enough to attract the attention of their scholars. There are, however, a few Cornish gleanings worth our attention; the place-name element *neved*, meaning a 'pagan sanctuary', can be detected in Lanivet and Carnevas, while at Bosence a votive offering was found to have been deposited in a well situated within an earthwork. In the 1940s a rough-worked Romano–Celtic stone idol was found on St Martin's, Isles of Scilly, and Charles Thomas has proposed that the islands take their collective name from a goddess, also commemorated at Bath, whose name began with *Sil* or *Sul*, and were in fact a centre of pagan pilgrimage.

Christianity first reached the British Isles in the second century but it is unlikely to have acquired a significant following until the end of the fourth. Its progress was often sporadic, with temporary periods of retreat, but by about 600 its position had become secure. Lewannick in the east and Phillack in the west were among the first Christian focal points in Cornwall, perhaps dating from the early fifth century, while there are also indications of early Christian influences being introduced from Gaul. Wales, and to a lesser extent Ireland, also made important contributions to the conversion of the Dumnonii throughout the Romano–Celtic period. The whole process is traditionally seen as a gradual one in which the new faith existed alongside paganism and,

*St Keyne's holy well*

28

indeed, absorbed many pagan traditions. The veneration of holy wells and pools continued, and heathen wells now became holy wells which were often renamed, like the famous well of St Keyne, after saints and hermits.

*The chi-rho monogram*

Evidence for the early Christian period is derived from a variety of sources which include standing stones, interments and place-name elements. In 1843 one of the earliest known Christian burials in Cornwall, dating from the fifth century, was discovered at Carnsew near Hayle. Here a grave 4 ft. below the surface was found to contain an inscribed stone which recorded the death of a certain 'Cunaide aged 33 years'. The progress of the new faith is also confirmed by the appearance of the so-called *chi-rho* monogram, a representation of the first two letters of the Greek word for Christ which was carved into a stone face. Early forms exist on a slab at Phillack which has been set into the wall on the south side of the church, while another, since lost, was recorded at Cape Cornwall in the 1870s. Later *chi-rho* forms are also known from St Endellion, South Hill and St Just, the latter being particularly interesting as the monogram appears on a small upright pillar discovered in 1834 and which also bears on its obverse the Latin inscription *Senilus Ic Iacet* – 'here lies Senilus'. This *hic iacit* formula, the product of continental influence, characterised very early Christian memorials although it tended to give way in the late sixth and seventh centuries to the *filius* inscription, introduced from Ireland, by which the deceased was styled as the 'son or daughter of' a named parent. A fine example stands in the churchyard at St Clement and bears the inscription *Vitali fili Torrici* – (the stone of) 'Vitalus the son of Torricus'.

How should we envisage the pattern and organisation of early Christian worship in Cornwall? The first requirement is to dispel any images of those sturdy granite churches and monasteries which characterised the medieval period and still grace the landscape of many communities. The first holy men lived as hermits in caves or rudimentary stone cells like the example excavated at St Helen's Oratory on the Scillies. With the appearance of the earliest religious communities would have come the erection of timber and wattle buildings which would not have looked out of place during the Iron Age. These would have been associated with cemeteries, although not always so, and in some instances abandoned 'rounds' appear to have been utilised for such purposes as may have been the case at Carnsew and St Buryan. The erection of inscribed memorials commemorating prominent figures, both lay and secular, would have contributed to raising the social prominence of these graveyard sites and, as the desire for communal Christian activity increased, simple stone chapels would be built within the cemetery perimeters. At this point, however, a note of caution needs to be sounded. It may well be a popularly held view that this sort of progression from burial site to Dark Age chapel and then to medieval church represents the normal model of ecclesiastical development

*Inscribed standing stone, St Just*

29

in the county, but archaeologists have been at pains to point out that surmise should not be allowed to replace hard evidence, and there are too many gaps in our knowledge for this to be more than an assumed pattern in many cases.

Cornwall has often been described as 'a land of saints', and no visitor to the county can fail to be impressed by the sheer range, not to mention the distinctive nomenclature, of the many holy figures commemorated in church dedications and place-names. The results of recent scholarship, however, have called into question some of the traditionally held assumptions about these figures and the part played by them in the conversion process. Partly because many saints' names duplicated in Wales, Ireland and Brittany, and partly because the many medieval 'Saints' Lives' frequently depict the first generation of holy men and women as some sort of pan-Celtic missionaries, it has become customary to envisage them endlessly traversing the western seaways, each founding a number of Christian communities and performing such wondrous acts that their cults spread throughout the Celtic world. While 'Saints' Lives' may make fascinating reading, however, their historical reliability is highly suspect; they were often written 500 years after the events they describe and only then with the express purpose of eulogising the 'founder' of a particular religious community. The frequency of supposed multiple dedications has also allowed conclusions to be made which are questioned by today's specialists. Take, for example, the figure of St Piran, patron saint of tin miners and more recently adopted as Cornwall's national saint. While few would accept the story that this sixth-century figure sailed across from Ireland on a millstone, he is repeatedly claimed to have established an oratory on the north coast at Perranzabuloe and given his name to Perranporth and Perranarworthel. While an oratory was discovered beneath the sands in 1835, it is unlikely to have been older than the ninth century and, in the absence of written evidence, it is quite impossible to claim that religious houses dedicated to St Piran or anyone else were actually founded by that saint, or, indeed, even refer to the same person. Even if we accept multiple dedications as commemorating a single individual and not several bearing indentical names, they probably represent the subsequent spread of a particular cult rather than reflect personal religious foundations. The many Cornish churches dedicated to Welsh saints, including St Breock, St Teath, St Mabyn, St Issey and St Endellion, are again best interpreted as indications of the importance of Welsh influences during the early Christian period rather than as houses actually founded by the individuals commemorated.

In all about 170 saints are honoured in Cornwall, including some native ones such as Just, Seleven and Constantine. About twenty are recorded in place-names which comprise the element *lann*, later *lan*, followed by a personal name. The term is equivalent to the Welsh *llan* and literally meant 'cemetery enclosure', although it is usually interpreted as indicating an early religious site, although this connection

*A reconstruction of St Piran's Oratory*

30

cannot be claimed with certainty in every case. The oldest spellings of Launceston took the form of *Lanstaphadon* indicating that this was the 'town of the church of St Stephen', while Landewednack on the Lizard represents the 'lan' of St Tewennoc. Other examples can be found in older place-name forms which are no longer in general usage; the church at St Keverne appears in the 11th century as *Lannachebran* and that at Perranzabuloe as *Lanpiran*. The village of Madron near Penzance is named after St Madernus and was originally known as *Landithy* while St Just-in-Roseland appears as *Lansioch* in 1202. The term *lann* also appears to be synonymous with a definite physical form, the raised, oval enclosures which represent early Christian grave-yards within which many churches were later erected. In some instances this distinctive oval shape has survived the centuries relatively unscathed and fine examples remain with the churchyards of Lewannick, Gulval and St Buryan.

It has become traditional to claim that the early Christian church in Cornwall was monastic in structure and that the list of religious houses recorded in Domesday Book represents communities established as early as the sixth and seventh centuries. In the absence of any documentary or archaeological evidence, however, such an interpretation is difficult to sustain, and in any case the distinction between church and monas-tery is essentially a medieval one which has little place in post-Roman Cornwall. Nonetheless, the Domesday evidence is the best insight we have into the number and distribution of early religious communities in the county. The port of Padstow takes its name from the 'stow' or 'place' of St Petroc, but the canons were subsequently obliged to move inland to Bodmin, a decision probably prompted by the Viking attacks of 981. As it transpired, the transfer proved beneficial with Bodmin outranking the other religious houses — Perranzabuloe, St Kew, St Carantoc, St Constantine, St Probus, St Neot's, St Keverne, St Buryan, St Germans and St Michael's Mount. There remains, finally, the contro-versial site at Tintagel which legend dictates was the birthplace of King Arthur. This rocky promontory has been excavated, interpreted and reinterpreted, although the most recent assessment favours a secular settlement rather than the traditional view that it should also be included in any list of early religious communities.

*Celtic cross
near St Buryan*

Before the assimilation of Cornwall into the newly united Kingdom of England the native Celtic church enjoyed a considerable degree of independence. It retained important differences in custom and practice from the Roman model adopted by the Anglo-Saxons, notably in the ritual of baptism, the shape of the monk's tonsure and, above all, in the method of calculating Easter. These issues had been fiercely debated at the Synod of Whitby in 663, a grand ecclesiastical gathering at which the Anglo-Saxons agreed to adopt Roman usages, but the Celtic church refused to follow suit. Most hostility was directed against the obstinate Welsh, but there is no reason to suppose that the Dumnonian Celts behaved differently or that they had begun to conform before the second half of the eighth century. The division of the county into parishes was also a late development and under the native system the territorial structure appears to have been rather amorphous, although it must be said that we know very little about the administrative structure of the Cornish church at this time. In the absence of documentary evidence we are obliged to look to Wales for a suitable model, and there the 10th-century Laws of Hywel Dda differentiated between the mother church or *clas* with its body of resident canons and the lesser church with its solitary priest. If the Cornish church had developed along similar lines, and the intimate cultural contacts with Wales make it hard to envisage otherwise, then we should regard houses like St Petroc's and Perranzabuloe as mother churches with a status also similar to the Anglo-Saxon minsters.

It is to the administrative innovations of Athelstan's reign that we should look for the widespread introduction of a parochial system in Cornwall, as before the early 10th century only the northern areas seem likely to have been affected. It should be appreciated that the absorption of the Celtic church into the see of Canterbury must have been a gradual process which echoed the hesitant nature of the Anglo-Saxon military conquest. After Egbert's victory over the Cornish at Hingston Down in 838 the Cornish bishop Kenstec was compelled to acknowledge the authority of Archbishop Ceolnoth. From Kenstec's letter of submission it is clear that his church remained 'monastic' in character, and on his death the bishop of Sherborne was commissioned to make annual visitations into Cornwall in order to 'uproot the errors' of the natives. In 909 Cornwall and Devon were united for ecclesiastical purposes into a single diocese centred on Crediton. Athelstan, perhaps anxious not to offend the sensibilities of the recently-conquered Cornish, made a conciliatory gesture by attaching a large endowment to the church of St Germans and making it the seat of a bishop to officiate 'west of the Tamar'. Moreover, by choosing a Cornishman, Conan, to fill this office, Athelstan made another gesture to native sentiment. Conan and his successors were auxiliary bishops acting on behalf of the Bishop of Crediton, and this pattern continued until 994 when King Aethelred made Cornwall into an independent diocese with its seat at St Germans. This arrangement, however, proved only temporary, and in *c.* 1027 Lyfing, abbot of Tavistock, was appointed Bishop of Crediton and subsequently Bishop of Cornwall as well. He began a process of consolidation which was completed after his death in 1046 when, under Bishop Leofric, the two dioceses of Devon and Cornwall were amalgamated. The seat of the united bishopric was fixed at Exeter, and in 1059 Edward the Confessor granted lands in St Keverne and St Martin-in-Meneague to Bishop Ealdred. Exeter was now to remain the ecclesiastical centre of the south-west until 1876 when Parliament sanctioned the creation of a new Cornish bishopric to be centred on Truro.

13. (*above*) Pelynt church, near Looe.

14. (*below*) Perranzabuloe church, built in 1804. Its medieval predecessor had to be abandoned to the encroaching sands but the impressive tower was dismantled and removed to the new site.

15. (*above*) The pilchard industry was a pillar of the Cornish economy throughout the 19th century. Once entrapped, the fish were 'tucked' to the surface with wicker baskets.

16. (*below*) Shipping at Padstow, *c.* 1890.

17. (*right*) Mending the nets at Newlyn: life for the fishing families was not always as idyllic as this photograph suggests.

18. (*below*) Landing fish at Newlyn harbour, near Penzance.

19. (*left*) Fishermen's cottages at St Ives at the turn of the century.

20. (*below*) St Ives fishermen 'tucking the seine'. Punts were frequently drawn up onto the gunwhales of the 'tuck boats' to prevent them from capsizing.

# IV Cornwall under the Normans

The decade which followed the Battle of Hastings in 1066 witnessed the gradual extension of Norman authority throughout England. These were turbulent times when William the Conqueror had to consolidate his position against a background of Saxon rebellion and Scandinavian claims to his newly-acquired throne. His reaction was momentous since he decided to dispossess most of the native landholders and redistribute their estates among those loyalists who had flocked to his standard in Normandy. The Anglo-Saxon Chronicle briefly recorded these moves under the year 1068: 'and he gave away every man's land when he came back' (from overseas). The chronicler, however, was evidently guilty of exaggeration, since in 1068 large areas of the country, including the south-west, still stood beyond the limits of Norman authority. In the same year a rebellion broke out in Exeter serious enough to warrant a royal expedition when the Conqueror himself is said to have marched into Cornwall. Soon afterwards most of Cornwall was granted to a Count Brian of Brittany, but he is an elusive figure and little is known about him; he fought at Hastings and took part in the 1068 campaign, but subsequently forfeited his lands after he took part in a baronial rebellion against the King in 1075. Soon after his lands in Cornwall and Devon were bestowed on a much more important figure, Robert, Count of Mortain. The great Domesday Survey of 1086 shows Robert to have been the holder of 277 Cornish manors, valued at £424, which virtually represented the whole of the county apart from a further 18 royal and 44 ecclesiastical estates.

Domesday Book, which was completed just before William the Conqueror's death, provides a fascinating insight into the society and economy of late 11th-century Cornwall. In the first place it reveals that the county was divided into seven (later nine) administrative districts known as hundreds, which were in turn controlled from a prominent estate which acted as the base of the hundredal bailiff. The farms, villages and hamlets within each hundred were then grouped into manors and about 340 are listed in the Cornish section. In many parts of the country the manor was a recognisable unit, but in Cornwall's case it is best seen as a term of administrative convenience which absorbed a diversity of settlements. In those areas which had experienced a great deal of Anglo-Saxon influence during the preceding two hundred years we find mainly large, nucleated manors bearing names which often contain the familiar suffixes of 'ham' and 'ton'.

*The two-lioned emblem of Normandy*

In hoc Manerio.ē mercatū in die dñico . ſed adnichilū redi
gitur ₚ mercato᷈mitis moritoñ qđ ibi.ē ₚximū.

120 d

Idē eṗs teñ *LANHERWEV*.T.R.E.geldb̄ ₚ.i.hida . ſed tam
ſt ibi.iii.hidæ.Tra.ē.x.caṙ.In dñio.ē.i.caṙ.⁊ iiii.ſerui.
⁊ viii.uilti ⁊ vi.borđ cū.iii.caṙ.Ibi paſtura.ii.leū lḡ.⁊ una
leū laṙ.Olim.c.ſoliđ.Modo ual.l.ſoliđ.Fulcard teñ⁷

Ricarđ teñ de eṗo *THINTEN*.T.R.E.geldb̄ ₚ diṁ hida.
Ibi taṁ.ē.i.hida.Tra.ē.vi.caṙ.In dñio.ē caṙ ⁊ dimiđ.
cū.i.ſeruo.⁊ v.uilti.⁊ ii.borđ cū.iii.caṙ.⁊ i.aꝯ ſiluæ.
Olim ⁊ modo ual.xxv.ſoliđ.

Ipſe eṗs teñ *LANGVITETONE*.T.R.E.geldb̄ ₚ.iiii.hiđ.
Ibi taṁ ſt.xi.hidæ.Tra.ē.xl.caṙ.In dñio ſt.ii.caṙ.
⁊ vii.ſerui.⁊ xxvii.uilti ⁊ xx.borđ cū xxix.caṙ.
Ibi.viii.aꝯ ṗti.⁊ c.aꝯ paſture.⁊ x.aꝯ ſiluæ minutæ.
Oli.viii.lib̄.Modo ual.xvii.lib̄.

Rolland teñ de eṗo *LANDICLE*.T.R.E.geldb̄ ₚ.i.hida.
Ibi taṁ.ē.i.hida ⁊ dimiđ.Tra.ē.xii.caṙ.In dñio.ē.i.caṙ.
⁊ iii.ſerui.⁊ xiii.uilti ⁊ iiii.borđ cū.iii.caṙ.Ibi.ii.aꝯ ṗti.
⁊ paſtura.ii.leū lḡ.⁊ una leū laṙ.Oli ⁊ modo ual.iii.lib̄.

Godefriđ teñ de eṗo *SANWINVEC*.T.R.E.geldb̄ ₚ.i.hida.
Tra.ē.vi.caṙ.In dñio.ē.i.caṙ.⁊ ii.ſerui.⁊ v.uilti ⁊ vi.borđ
cū.ii.caṙ.Ibi paſtura diṁ leū lḡ.⁊ tñtđ laṙ.Silua dimiđ
leū lḡ.⁊ una qᷱ laṙ.Olim.xl.ſol.Modo ual.xx.ſoliđ.

De æccła S̄ Germani ablata.ē.i.hida træ.q̄ reddeb̄ p c̄ſue
tudiñ unā cupā ceruiſæ ⁊ xxx.denaṙ T.R.E.eiđ æccłæ
De eađ æccła.ē ablata.i.aꝯ træ.⁊ ē tra.i.caṙ.
De eađ æccła.ē ablata.i.virg træ. ⎩lin de comite moriṫ.

Ħ erant T.R.E.in dñio ejđ æccłæ.Modo teñ Rainalđ ⁊ Hame
Oᴍꜱ ʜᴀꜱ ᴛʀᴀs tenuit Leuric eṗs T.R.E.

Fig. 1. A page from the Domesday Survey of Cornwall. The text of
Domesday Book was printed first in 1783 in an edition by Abraham
Farley. These pages have been reproduced from the edition published
by Phillimore & Co. Ltd., with Farley's original text and a modern
English translation.

34

In this manor there is a market on Sunday, but it is reduced
to nothing by the Count of Mortain's market which is nearby,
in a castle of his, on the same day.

E

7  LANHERNE. Before 1066, it paid tax for 1 h;but 3 h. there,however.120 d
   Land for 10 ploughs; in lordship 1 plough; 4 slaves; 1 v.
       8 villagers and 6 smallholders with 3 ploughs & 2 h. 3 v.  200
       Pasture, 2 leagues long and 1 league wide.  a 1
   Formerly 100s; value now 50s.
   Fulchard holds from the Bishop.

8  Richard holds TINTEN from the Bishop. Before 1066 it paid
   tax for ½ h; 1 h. there, however. Land for 6 ploughs;
   in lordship 1½ ploughs, with 1 slave; 1 v.  200
       5 villagers and 2 smallholders with 3 ploughs & 3 v.  b 1
       Woodland, 1 acre.
   Value formerly and now 25s. 3 cattle; 20 sheep.

9  The Bishop himself holds LAWHITTON. Before 1066 it paid
   tax for 4 h; 11 h. there, however. Land for 40 ploughs;  200
   in lordship 2 ploughs; 7 slaves; 1 h.  b 2
       27 villagers and 20 smallholders with 29 ploughs & 10 h.
       Meadow, 8 acres; pasture, 100 acres; underwood, 10 acres.
   Formerly £8; value now £17. 1 cob; 2 cows; 40 sheep.

10 Roland holds GULVAL from the Bishop. Before 1066 it paid  E
   tax for 1 h; 1½ h. there, however. Land for 12 ploughs;  200
   in lordship 1 plough; 3 slaves; 1 v.  b 3
       13 villagers and 4 smallholders with 3 ploughs & 1 h. 3 v.
       Meadow, 2 acres; pasture, 2 leagues long and 1 league wide.
   Value formerly and now £3. 1 cob; 3 cows; 30 sheep.

11 Godfrey holds ST. WINNOW from the Bishop. Before 1066 it paid  201
   tax for 1 h. Land for 6 ploughs; in lordship 1 plough; 2 slaves; 1 v.  a 1
       5 villagers and 6 smallholders with 2 ploughs & 3 v.
       Pasture, ½ league long and as wide; woodland, ½ league
           long and 1 f. wide.
   Formerly 40s; value now 20s. 30 sheep.

12 From ST. GERMAN'S Church 1 h. of land has been taken away; it  201
   paid 1 barrel of ale and 30d to this Church by custom before 1066.  a 2-4

13 From this Church 1 acre of land has been taken away. Land for 1 plough.

14 From this Church 1 v. of land has been taken away.
   They were in the lordship of this Church before 1066. Now Reginald  E
   and Hamelin hold them from the Count of Mortain.

15 Bishop Leofric held all these lands before 1066.

Not surprisingly, the majority in this category are to be found in the eastern part of the county between the Tamar and Lynher rivers. Elsewhere, however, the picture is quite different, because in the traditionally Celtic areas the manor seems to have been little more than an artificial, bureaucratic term for an area which might include a number of unnamed villages as well as many isolated farmsteads. In general the Celtic manors were mainly pastoral, while much more arable farming was carried out in the more efficiently organised Anglo-Saxon estates.

*An 11th-century ploughman*

The Domesday commissioners were asked to provide a wealth of information on each manor, including what it was worth, who controlled it, how many workers lived in it, and what livestock and other assets it contained. The manor of Liskeard will serve as a suitable example of Norman thoroughness; we are told that before the Conquest it was held by a certain Maerleswegn (sheriff of Lincolnshire), and that its value had risen from £8 to £26. It contained a working male population of 92, and its economic assets consisted of a mill, a market, 300 acres of woodland, 8 square leagues of pasture, 250 sheep, 10 cattle, 8 horses and 3 ploughteams. By analysing statistics like these for all of Cornwall's 340 manors we can reconstruct a reliable picture of the county at the end of King William's reign. The first conclusion is that this was a land of relative poverty. The most prosperous and heavily populated parts were the far north, the eastern parishes bordering the Tamar valley, and the coastal strip between Plymouth and Mevagissey. The most valuable, Stratton, was worth £36 but over one-third were worth only £1 or less. Most estates, moreover, had experienced a serious decline in their fortunes since the Conquest, and this is reflected not only in their values but in the fact that over two-thirds were exempt from the payment of geld or tax. In all, about 5,500 working males are recorded, suggesting a total population of about 27,000, although this meant an average of below five people per square mile. Over twenty per cent, moreover, were classified as serfs or slaves as against nine per cent for the rest of the country, and a high ratio of serfs is generally regarded as a barometer of economic backwardness. As the great scholar of Norman England, F. W. Maitland, observed, 'every test we can apply shows the extreme poverty of the country that once was West Wales'.

While the motives behind the Domesday Survey were many and varied, the final record was not intended to be an economic census. For that reason it does not provide a complete picture and nothing, for example, was recorded about the Cornish tin industry or the extent of fishing. The survey is also relatively uninformative on the subject of early towns, something we would like to know much more about. It seems logical to assume that some communities had been gradually developing urban characteristics and functions since late Anglo-Saxon times, but Domesday provides only a hint of this. Only one settlement, in fact, was worth noting, Bodmin with 68 houses, although the entry for Launceston suggests an embryonic borough. Since it was not the brief of the Domesday commissioners to record all existing towns, however, we can assume that others may have been hidden under the cloak of manorialism. Padstow and Kilkhampton seem likely candidates while Helston, listed as a royal manor whose 40 men paid a tax in ale, must also be a probability. Neither should we expect to find a full picture of religious life in the folios as churches only appear if they were landholders, and so the majority were unworthy of notice. Nonetheless, it is quite clear that the Norman settlement had caused great disturbance to the old Celtic houses which were still adjusting to the recently imposed authority of Canterbury. It is clear that they were extremely vulnerable to spoliation and none more so than St Petroc's which had lost 10 manors. The Canons of St Piran, St Kew and St Carantoc also suffered, and we are left with the conclusion that accidentally but unarguably the Normans delivered the *coup de grâce* to the old Celtic church which was now deprived of an adequate economic base. Many religious houses now became dependencies of other foundations, including St Carantoc, St Neot's, St Caroc's and Altarnon which were granted to the Somerset priory of Montacute, and St Michael's Mount which passed to its Norman counterpart, Mont St Michel. Likewise the church at Fowey was granted to the new priory of Black Monks at Tywardreath which had been founded by Richard fitz Turold.

Fig. 2. An early 19th-century print of Mawnan church.

Domesday Book also provides evidence of the tenurial revolution which had followed in the wake of the Conquest. Before the arrival of the Normans most of Cornwall's manors had been controlled either by members of the royal family or by a number of prominent figures like Maerleswegn, the former sheriff of Lincoln. As we have already seen, however, most of the pre-Conquest tenants were dispossessed and two-thirds of all the lands passed to William the Conqueror's half-brother, Count Robert of Mortain.

Robert of Mortain was an important figure who had been in the foreground of political events in both England and Normandy since the early 1060s. A few years before the Conquest he had been entrusted with the Norman fief of Mortain and he is supposed to have contributed as many as 120 ships to William's invasion force. He fought at Hastings, and the famous Bayeux Tapestry depicts him as seated on the Conqueror's left with his sword half-drawn. Robert's support was generously rewarded, and by 1086 he held over a thousand English manors, valued at more than £2,000 and distributed throughout 20 counties. Many of his estates were concentrated in the south-west and in Cornwall his position was clearly exceptional. Some writers, in fact, have gone so far as to argue that he was actually Earl of Cornwall but there is no reliable evidence to support this assertion as he is not styled as such in any contemporary document. Of the 277 Cornish manors in his possession Robert retained the most profitable for himself as his demesne. Although this only amounted to 22 estates, their combined value was £243 which represents more than half of the total Mortain interest in the county. Moreover, the value of this select group had risen substantially since the Conquest, when the overall trend was one of decline, while two manors, Stratton and Liskeard, were alone worth an impressive £62. The remainder were entrusted to a variety of sub-tenants and the Survey records the names of over forty. Surprisingly, some 28 were Anglo-Saxons, but as a group they were well down the social ladder and held only 67 impoverished manors between them. Most had been landholders before the Conquest but had experienced substantial dispossession; a certain Alric for example, now kept only two of his previous 21 estates and had seen the combined value of his tenancy fall from £17 to a mere 11s. 0d. Three, possibly four, Bretons are also listed; Wihomarch, Bloyou, Briend, and perhaps Alvred, although his nationality is in doubt. Alvred was Count Robert's *pincerna* or household steward and he had evidently been well rewarded for his service with lands throughout the four south-western counties. A solitary Fleming, Erchenbald, also appears as the tenant of two manors including Brea in St Just, which was still in the family in 1228 when it was held by Archibald 'le Flemag'. All these men, however — Saxons, Bretons and Flemings — were clearly minor figures in the Cornish feudal hierarchy because Count Robert entrusted the remaining 155 manors into the hands of a select band of 12 Norman followers of whom the most important was Richard fitz Turold. Richard controlled

*A Norman knight from the Bayeux Tapestry*

38

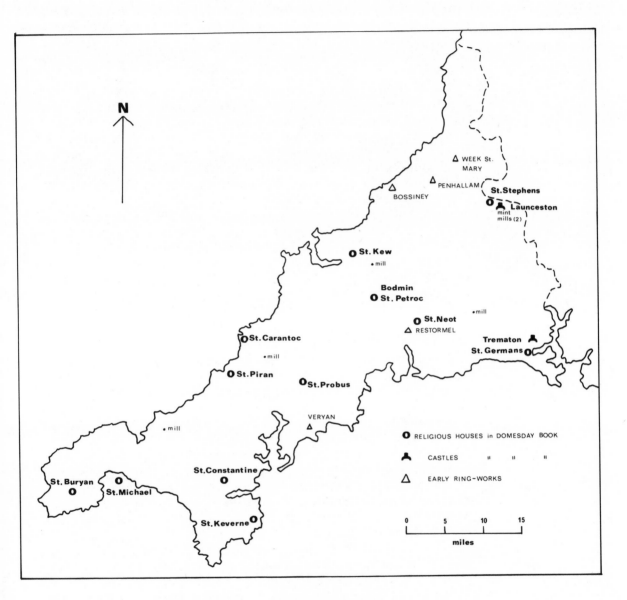

N

WEEK St. MARY

PENHALLAM

BOSSINEY

St.Stephens

O ▲ Launceston
mint
mills (2)

O St.Kew
• mill

Bodmin
O St.Petroc
• mill

O St.Neot
△ RESTORMEL

O St.Carantoc

Trematon ▲
St.Germans O

• mill

O St.Piran

O St.Probus

VERYAN
△

O RELIGIOUS HOUSES in DOMESDAY BOOK

▲ CASTLES   ˮ    ˮ    ˮ

△ EARLY RING-WORKS

• mill

St.Constantine
O

St.Buryan
O

O
St.Michael

St.Keverne O

0        5        10        15

miles

Norman Cornwall.

39

a fee of 29 estates and he seems to have been an important figure in the overall administration of the county. Also prominent was Reginald de Valletort who held lands from Count Robert in Normandy as well. Reginald controlled a large, compact fee concentrated in north-east Cornwall and stretching across the Tamar into the South Hams area of Devon. His base was at Trematon where he constructed a castle to control the upper reaches of the Tamar estuary. The Domesday Survey also reveals the identity of the county's earliest known sheriff, Turstin, who had been granted 24 manors which subsequently passed to his son Baldwin.

The Norman administration in Cornwall was centred on two important castles, Trematon, already mentioned, and Dunheved Castle at Launceston, which Count Robert built on land exchanged with the Bishop of Exeter. Initially this would have been a timber affair and the impressive stone structure which became known as 'Castle Terrible' is unlikely to have been started until the mid-12th century, probably during Reginald de Dunstanville's tenure of the Cornish earldom, 1141–1175. The Count also had a market and a mill here, while another market had been established at Trematon much to the despair, we are told, of the monks of St German's whose own market had consequently been 'reduced to nothing'. Although Trematon and Launceston are the only fortifications recorded in the Cornish Domesday archaeologists have identified several other ringwork castles dating from this period, at Penhallam, Bossiney, Restormel and Week St Mary. That at Penhallam seems to have been the most important, functioning as the headquarters of Richard fitz Turold's lands until his descendants built a more substantial castle at Cardinham in or about 1200.

*Launceston Castle*

Leaving statistics and sub-tenants behind, it is worth speculating as to what the arrival of the Normans would have meant to the ordinary people of Cornwall. Few tears are likely to have been shed over the dispossession of the alien Saxons, but at the same time one ruling class had simply been replaced by another. One thing, however, is certain; whereas the Anglo-Saxon conquest had been followed by substantial colonisation, if confined to the north of the county, the Norman Conquest was not. Theirs was an aristocratic take-over and many even of the new landholders probably lived elsewhere, making only occasional visits to their estates. It would be wrong, in fact, to envisage the Norman presence in Cornwall beyond that of a few hundred administrators, castle-wardens, monks and merchants. To the vast majority of the new Norman overlords the remoteness of Cornwall cannot have made it an attractive place in which to settle. The natives must have seemed a strange commodity who spoke a peculiar language and who were probably not to be trusted; to one early 12th-century chronicler, William of Malmesbury, Cornwall was a land whose inhabitants amounted to no more than a 'contaminated race'.

Count Robert of Mortain died in or about 1090 when his lands in Cornwall and elsewhere passed to his son, William. In 1106, however,

40

William was dispossessed for his part in a baronial rebellion against Henry I. The rebels were defeated at the Battle of Tinchebrai in Normandy and the Anglo-Saxon Chronicle recorded that 'William . . . worked against the King, for which reason the King deprived him of everything and confiscated what he had in this country'. This now meant that new arrangements had to be made with his sub-tenants, and in Cornwall many were elevated to the position of tenants-in-chief, holding their lands directly from the Crown. Some fees were in turn amalgamated to form the substantial 'honours' which dominated the Cornish feudal scene throughout the next two hundred years. Among the largest was the Honour of Launceston Castle, which was made up of all the Domesday manors of Erchenbald the Fleming plus those of another sub-tenant, Hamelin. Likewise Richard fitz Turold's 29 Cornish estates were combined with his five Devonshire manors into the Honour of Cardinham, which continued to be held by his lineal descendants until the late 13th century. Again, the vast Domesday fee of Reginald de Valletort emerged as the Honour of Trematon and continued in the family until 1270 when it passed to Richard of Cornwall. Such continuity was also repeated further down the social order; five of the six manors held by Bloyou the Breton in 1086 were still in the hands of his descendants three centuries later. The association of the Mortain family with Cornwall may have been short-lived, but the legacy of the Norman settlement proved to be much more durable.

# V Medieval Cornwall

The stability and order which had characterised the first half-century of Norman rule came to an abrupt end with the death of Henry I in 1135. His son and heir had died 15 years earlier and two principal contenders, his daughter Mathilda and nephew Stephen, crowned in December 1135, now laid claim to the throne and plunged England into a civil war which was to divide the nation for more than a decade. Throughout the country the baronial classes aligned themselves with one or other of the claimants, sometimes changing sides as their respective fortunes ebbed and flowed, and as Stephen's position gradually became stronger. Although the position of Cornwall during these years is far from clear, several 'adulterine' castles were hastily built, including possibly the strongholds at Truro and Kilkhampton, which are usually taken as indications of disorder. Stephen appointed the important William fitz Richard of Cardinham as his county lieutenant, but William switched his allegiance to Mathilda and took Launceston Castle. The King responded by despatching a force to oust him and then entrusted the administration of the county to Count Alan of Brittany. Stephen died in 1154 and his successor, Henry of Anjou, found Alan unacceptable and granted the earldom of Cornwall to his uncle, Richard.

With the restoration of order under Henry II came great administrative advances and the increasing sophistication of government record-keeping enables us to construct a much clearer picture of events in Cornwall during the late 12th and 13th centuries. The county was now an earldom, although uncertainty still surrounds the antiquity of this office and attempts to place it in the early Norman period or even earlier have been far from successful. In the *Life* of St Rumon, the patron saint of Tavistock Abbey, we are told that the abbey's 10th-century founder, Ordulf, was also 'earl of Cornwall', but this should not be taken as anything more than a later attempt to add extra dignity to his person. As we have also seen in the previous chapter, equal uncertainty surrounds Brian of Brittany and Robert of Mortain who dominated the Cornish tenurial scene in the late 11th century. Both have been credited from time to time with the status of earl but the evidence is really very flimsy. At all events, the office had definitely become a reality by the middle of the 12th century and the title and lands were generally bestowed on a member of the royal family. In 1189 Prince John was granted possession of Cornwall, with the exception of Launceston Castle which remained in the hands of the king.

*Dupath holy well*

42

In 1225 Henry III granted the earldom to his younger brother who was universally known as Richard of Cornwall, while from 1272–1300 the title was held by his son, Edmund. Edmund died childless and the earldom passed into the hands of Edward I and then to Edward II who bestowed it on his court favourite, Piers Gaveston, in August 1307. In 1312, however, Gaveston was executed and for the next 25 years the earldom saw a succession of holders which seems to have had an adverse effect on the prosperity of its estates; when Edward III came to the throne he resolved to carry out a major reorganisation. Accordingly, in 1337 in a full session of Parliament, he created the Duchy of Cornwall for the maintenance of his eldest son, Edward the Black Prince, and the title was now automatically to pass to the first-born son of the monarch. The Duchy lands have never been solely confined to Cornwall, but during the medieval period the Cornish holdings were the main core, consisting of 17 manors together with the boroughs of Camelford, Grampound, Helston, Launceston, Liskeard, Lostwithiel, Tintagel, Trematon and Saltash. The Duke was also given a variety of other financial benefits including the profits of the county courts, control of wrecks, and the right to collect a duty of £2 on each 1,000 lbs. of tin.

*The Arms of Richard of Cornwall*

Earls and dukes, however, were distant figures, often absentee landlords rarely, if ever, seen by many of the ordinary people of Cornwall. More important to them were the numerous officials who administered the everyday concerns of local government, justice and taxation. For these purposes the county was divided into the seven hundreds of Penwith, Kerrier, Pydar, Powder, East and West Wivel and Trigg. The latter was subsequently trisected to create the additional hundreds of Lesnewth and Stratton. Each hundred was centred on a dominant manor, some were in royal hands while others, like Penwith, were private hundreds; Richard of Cornwall granted it to John of Conarton and subsequently it passed to the Arundell family. Every hundred, royal or private, was administered by a bailiff who was responsible to the County Sheriff. In Cornwall the office of hundredal bailiff was hereditary and was associated with the tenure of a certain piece of land. The bailiff's function was primarily to collect monies due to the King and to administer the hundredal court which usually met every three or four weeks. The duties of his superior, the sheriff, were considerable and had been steadily increasing since late Saxon times; he dealt with the arrest and custody of criminals, the summoning of the local militia, distraining of goods, collecting royal revenue from a variety of sources, as well as supervising the monthly County Court and the twice-yearly Tourn which dealt with petty offences. Not surprisingly, the execution of these duties often made sheriffs unpopular figures, particularly as they frequently had to deal with offenders by distraining animals which were then kept in pounds until the account was settled. During the 1270s Roger de Carnyon operated the sheriff's pound in Kerrier and had the right to demand one penny for each animal held.

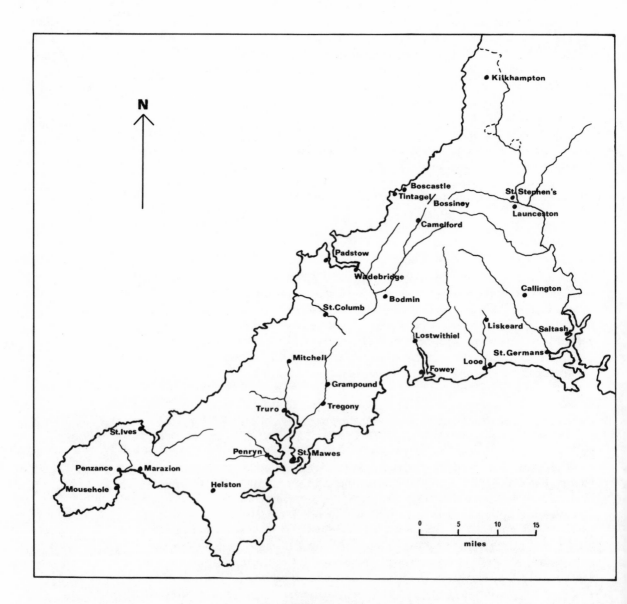

N

Kilkhampton

Boscastle
Tintagel
Bossiney
Camelford

St.Stephen's
Launceston

Padstow
Wadebridge
Bodmin
St.Columb

Callington

Lostwithiel
Liskeard
Saltash
St.Germans

Mitchell
Fowey
Looe

Grampound
Truro
Tregony

St.Ives
Penryn
St.Mawes

Penzance
Marazion
Mousehole
Helston

0    5    10    15
miles

Cornwall's medieval towns and boroughs.

44

At the local level the manor was the unit of administration and minor disputes were dealt with by the manorial courts. Here the chief official was the reeve who in Cornwall was elected on an annual basis. Finally, there came that uniquely Cornish institution, the Stannary Courts. During the second half of the 12th century the tin industry had enjoyed one of its periodic booms and in 1201 King John granted a royal charter exempting tinners from normal laws and taxes, and allowed them the right to search for tin on common land. The charter divided the county into four districts or stannaries, which then held their own courts for those involved in the industry and maintained a separate gaol at Lostwithiel. Each stannary, moreover, appointed six stannators who met periodically in the so-called 'Tinners Parliament' to discuss issues of interest and concern; it last sat officially as late as 1752, and in recent years there have been attempts to revive it as a manifestation of Cornish nationality.

Throughout the early medieval period the centre of administration for the whole county was the borough of Launceston, where a castle had been built in the late 11th century. This structure was subsequently rebuilt and enlarged, and arrangements were made for it to be garrisoned by wardens who were assigned lands in return for serving periods of castle guard. In 1210, for example, John de Pencoit held 1½ acres as long as he performed his annual spell of 15 days on duty and arrived 'with sack and lance'. During the mid-13th century, however, Lostwithiel came to challenge Launceston's supremacy as it was chosen as the administrative centre of first the Earldom and then the Duchy. There was no castle at Lostwithiel itself, although these years saw the construction of a completely new stronghold at nearby Restormel, which was probably begun by Robert of Cardinham in about 1200. Earl Richard of Cornwall purchased the castle from Ysolda of Cardinham and his successor Earl Edmund made it his chief place of residence in the county. Trematon Castle, the home of the de Valletorts, also seems to have been rebuilt during this period which also saw the construction of Botreaux Castle at Boscastle.

*Trematon Castle gateway*

Throughout the Middle Ages farming remained the mainstay of the Cornish economy and the manor the main agricultural unit. At the time of the Domesday Survey there were about 340 manors in the county but these varied tremendously in their size, populations and economic condition. The convenient administrative label of 'manor' also disguised important variations in the nature of medieval settlement. It has been traditional to envisage the medieval Cornish landscape as having consisted of two contrasting patterns of grouped and dispersed holdings representing the respective influences of Saxon and Celtic cultures. According to this model, nucleated villages were to be found in the Saxonised eastern parishes and around the larger towns, while elsewhere manors may have contained hundreds of separate farmsteads which reflected the Celtic distaste for grouped communities. While there is undoubtedly much to be said for this contrasting image of the

Cornish landscape modern research warns us against making too rigid a distinction. Professor Beresford analysed Duchy of Cornwall records for five representative parishes during the 13th and 14th centuries and, while he concluded that most villages were in or near Saxonised areas, the idea of the absolutely isolated holding elsewhere is fairly unrepresentative. Overall, only one house in 20 stood completely alone and the pattern was more of a landscape of small clusters of dwellings. Investigation into field patterns has also contributed to a clearer understanding of the medieval countryside. The emphasis of earlier historians on a supposed patchwork of isolated farmsteads led to an assumption that the open-field system of farming, whereby peasants worked several strips or 'stitches' irregularly distributed in large common fields, was not introduced into Cornwall. Recent research, however, has categorically shown that open-fields were common to the county, although the important qualification is that they were largely concentrated around the main boroughs where English influences were strongest. Fossilised remains of these strips can still be detected around the old boroughs of Grampound and Marazion, while the best examples are the Forrabury Stitches at Boscastle where 40 strips can still be identified. Place-name evidence is also instructive in this respect as the Cornish word *guel*, commonly written *gweal* and meaning an open-field, can be found in the vicinity of many old towns, including Truro, Penryn and Helston. Again, detailed study by N. J. G. Pounds of over 250 land utilization maps, known as the 'Lanhydrock Atlas', also confirmed the adoption of the open-field system, and he found it even to have been a feature of remote western communities like St Just, where 31 'stitches' were marked. Archaeologists, too, have made their contribution and investigation of the site of a medieval village at Garrow Tor on Bodmin Moor further reinforced the conclusion that open-fields could also be found well away from centres of English influence. Although, then, this pattern was evidently common, nevertheless it remains the case that many areas did not adopt it, and there is no record, for example, of open-field agriculture being practised on any of the 17 Duchy manors at any time during the medieval period. For many homesteads and hamlets the much older 'in and out-field' system operated, by which dwellings were surrounded by arable lands and meadow with belts of pasture lying beyond. While much research into Cornish settlement patterns remains to be carried out, the important point is that we should not be misled into envisaging a stereotyped picture of the medieval landscape.

Throughout medieval Cornwall a system of mixed farming predominated, although in the eastern parishes there was greater emphasis on the keeping of livestock. The place-name element *hendre*, which came to signify a 'winter farmstead', indicates that transhumance was common with livestock being moved onto upland moors during the summer months and transferred to lowland pasture at the onset of winter. The main arable crops were wheat and oats while barley, rye

*A medieval labourer harvesting the crop*

46

and peas were also popular. Land used for cultivation was periodically left to lie fallow and to provide grazing which would then benefit from natural manuring. Fertility was also increased by the addition of sea-sand, rich in calcium carbonate, and by the practice of 'beat-burning', by which dry turves were piled up and burnt and the potash-bearing ashes spread prior to ploughing. On coastal farms it was also common to add seaweed and fish to the land, a practice still carried out in some areas. Woodland was also a vital element of the medieval economy providing fuel, charcoal, grazing or 'pannage' for pigs, and was accordingly regarded as an important manorial asset. Cornwall at this time had more woodland than it has today, although the Domesday commissioners only recorded its presence on less than 60 per cent of the county's manors. Their record was not comprehensive, however, and later evidence considered in the light of place-names suggests that they noted only the largest and most valuable areas. Nevertheless, the widespread use of timber for building, fuel, fencing and tin mining had produced a shortage by the 15th century when Duchy officials were forced to initiate a conservation policy. Such a modern approach, though, met with only limited success, and it is clear that many tenants continued to fell trees and steal the Duke's wood, as they also did his deer. Deer-hunting was a favourite sport of the feudal aristocracy, and in Cornwall the Duchy had seven deer-parks, the largest with 300 deer being Restormel near its Lostwithiel base. In practice, however, generations of poachers seem to have made greater use of these parks than did the dukes and their attendants.

*A medieval salt-works*

Under the medieval tenurial system the holding of land was linked to a variety of services and obligations, some military, others involving varying degrees of labour-service. At the top of the feudal ladder the large Honours like Launceston and Cardinham were expected to provide a quota of knights for the Crown which was determined by mutual agreement. Others, as we have already seen, held their estates in return for performing periodic spells of castle-guard. Further down the social order came a variety of tenurial categories which reflected an individual's degree of freedom. On those lands belonging to the Duchy, tenants were grouped into three categories, conventionary tenants paid a fixed rent and were obliged to perform a variety of specified services but they had no right of automatic renewal of their tenancy. Then came the free tenants who paid a fairly low annual rental and their heirs could succeed them on payment of a small sum to the Duke. Finally there were the villeins who held their lands by hereditary right and paid a fixed rent, although their possessions technically belonged to the Duke. The villeins had become an increasingly servile class and the late 12th century, in particular, had seen the fairly rapid loss of peasant legal freedoms. Villeins could not, for example, give away their daughters in marriage without making a payment to the Duke, nor could they send their sons to school or into the Church without his permission. They were also expected to

47

*A medieval windmill*

perform 'week work' which meant labouring on the lord's lands for a fixed number of days each week, although as the 13th century progressed the practice of commutation, by which a tenant could pay a cash sum in lieu of labour service, became increasingly common. The conditions of villeinage varied considerably throughout the country and local circumstances dictated different obligations on different manors; at Climsland they were obliged to supply Launceston Castle with wood, while the villeins of Calstock had to carry mill-stones — no mean task — to the lord's mill when required.

Throughout the medieval period farming remained the principal provider of employment and wealth. It has been traditional to regard the Cornish economy during these centuries as weak and to see the poverty suggested by the Domesday evidence as continuing throughout the Middle Ages. In his detailed study of the Duchy records, however, John Hatcher has warned against over-generalisation, pointing to the need to consider the numerous other sources of wealth which often lay beyond the scope of medieval taxation and so rarely figured in the normal returns. Little documentary evidence, for example, has survived of fishing during this period, although it is impossible to imagine that it was not widespread. The 16th-century antiquary John Norden noted that the Cornish waters had 'greate store and manie kindes of verie excellent fishe' and we know that a not inconsiderable £1,000-worth had been exported in 1438, not to mention that which was consumed locally or sent to other parts of the country. At this time hake was the most important species, although by the 16th century the fish had changed its migratory habits and had been replaced by pilchards. Oysters and salmon were also common, while freshwater fisheries were greatly coveted and many weirs were constructed along the river courses to trap eels, salmon and trout. The growth of the tin industry also illustrates the increasing diversity of the Cornish economy, although during the early medieval period west Devon was a far more important producer than Cornwall. The expansion of the industry in the late 13th and early 14th centuries, however, is associated with a progressive move westwards, and by the 1330s as much as 1,650 million lbs. of ore was being presented for coinage each year; there was also a flourishing black market in existence by this time. These were boom years for the tinners, but like everyone else their economic and social foundations were to be rocked by the traumas of the notorious Black Death.

The Black Death, or 'Great Pestilence' as it was originally known, was caused mainly, though not entirely, by bubonic plague which originated in what is now Russian central Asia and was quickly carried by rats across the trade routes of Europe. It first arrived in England in 1348 by way of Melcombe Regis in Dorset and quickly spread throughout the south-west, reaching Cornwall in the spring of the following year. By 1351 tin production had fallen by 80 per cent and farm tenants found themselves unable to meet their rents, with holdings falling vacant for want of takers; Moresk manor was typical with 23

*Early Cornish tinners, from a 16th-century woodcut*

48

21. (*above*) The legendary site of King Arthur's castle, Tintagel.

22. (*below*) Mousehole harbour.

23. (*above*) Levant Mine, situated on the cliffs near Pendeen on the western tip of Cornwall.

24. (*left*) An underground view of East Pool Mine, Redruth, *c.* 1890.

25. (*right*) Men waiting to descend Cornwall's deepest mine at Dolcoath, near Camborne, *c.* 1890.

26. (*below*) Miners at East Pool pictured taking their 'croust' or snack, *c.* 1890.

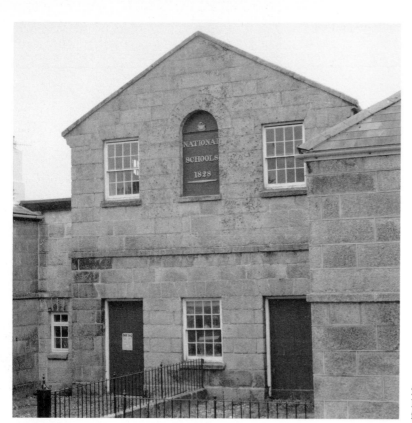

27. (*left*) The former National School at Helston, built in 1828 by the Church authorities.

28. (*below*) Flower growers on the Isles of Scilly, preparing their blooms for market.

vacant holdings out of a total of fifty. Landlords found themselves forced to reduce rents to increase incentive, but even then a shortage of labour meant that large areas of arable land were allowed to revert to pasture. Historians still argue over the national extent of fatalities but the traditional figure of about one-third of the total population is still generally accepted. The Cornish evidence is not particularly illuminating but a useful indication is provided by the numbers of priests appointed to new benefices since the clergy were as vulnerable as most; throughout the first 40 years of the 14th century an average of about ten priests was appointed each year but at the height of the Pestilence in 1350–1 the figure had risen to eighty. Some more remote communities were so badly affected that the combination of fatalities and consequent labour shortages forced the survivors to abandon them completely. Upland villages were particularly affected in this way, like Tresmorn on the north coast where 15 dwellings were left to the elements.

*A scene from an allegory of the Black Death*

While the Black Death had obvious catastrophic human consequences, its long-term economic effects should not be exaggerated. The older impression of the late 14th and early 15th centuries as a period of economic decline, falling rents and urban decay is now treated with caution, and in Cornwall the Pestilence had drastic immediate effects but in the long-term its impact was marginal. Though a second outbreak of plague hit the county in 1360–2, tin production had recovered by the 1380s and the population of 55,000 suggested by the Poll Tax returns suggests that there was enough work to attract new labourers from beyond the Tamar. It was this very diversity of the economy, in fact, which cushioned Cornwall from the worst effects of the catastrophe. Apart from tin, fishing and slate-quarrying were making an increasingly important contribution, while the eastern parishes were beginning to benefit from the advent of textile manufacturing. During the first half of the 15th century the export of cloths from Cornish ports increased almost ten-fold and the proliferation of place-names like 'Tuckingmill' or the Cornish equivalent *Melindruckya* remain as a testimony to this expansion. A 'tuckingmill' was the west-country term for a fulling-mill, where the cloth was treated and prepared for market, and the Cornish historian Charles Henderson identified nearly sixty such sites by analysing place-name forms. The boroughs of Lostwithiel and St Germans were also renowned for their pottery production, and the growth of these non-agrarian sectors of the Cornish economy should not be underestimated, since any depression in farming would only have induced many people to pursue a number of occupations, concentrating on one according to varying market demands. Analysis of the Duchy tenants, in fact, reveals that many were also tinners, fishermen, blacksmiths and fullers, and with so many holdings under ten acres this sort of variation was an absolute necessity for many families.

In the countryside the Black Death had one beneficial effect for ordinary people, in that it contributed to a decline in peasant servility,

*A medieval merchant*

49

even though in the short term the shortage of labour led landlords to assert their customary rights over their tenants. While this caused friction it was doomed to failure and the old villein class owing labour service to the lords was becoming increasingly reluctant to accept this servility. Money rents began to replace labour rents and the more secure form of copyhold tenure, by which the tenant was able to obtain a copy of his terms of service, had become the norm by the end of the 15th century. In Cornwall copyhold tenure normally gave security for three lives, the people preferring to negotiate by generations rather than by a fixed number of years. The pace of this transition varied from manor to manor, however, and it also took place against a background of economic fluctuations. The Cornish economy suffered another reversal at the end of the century as a result of a national trade slump which was immediately felt. The demand for land again declined with a consequent fall in rents, particularly in the far west where the Duchy was obliged to offer cash discounts to tenants prepared to repair their own farm buildings. Tin production again dropped although not by anywhere near the drastic levels of the 1340s. The conclusion, though few would have drawn it at the time, was that Cornwall and its economy had been drawn into the wider commercial orbit not only of England but of Europe. Centuries of virtual independence were unbeknowingly coming to an end and the process was about to accelerate as the eventful 16th century progressed.

# VI  Medieval Towns and Churches

The growth of towns came relatively late to Cornwall, and before the middle of the 12th century few settlements had assumed urban characteristics or functions. Unfortunately the early history of the county's towns is poorly documented and the picture is further complicated by the fact that historians have been unable to agree on a common interpretation of the little that is known about their origins and early development. The traditional view, advanced by the late Charles Henderson and others, follows the argument that the Cornish, like their Welsh cousins, showed a cultural reluctance towards nucleated settlements, preferring a landscape made up of small hamlets and scattered farmsteads. Towns were consequently the result of Norman and Angevin influences, and they cite the negative evidence of an early 10th-century document known as the 'Burghal Hidage' which does not list a single town in the whole of the county. To Henderson, towns were mainly 'planted' as the artificial creations of speculative Anglo-Norman barons, who saw in them potential sources of wealth and prestige. More recent writers, however, while accepting the important rôle played by these landholders in granting legal and commercial privileges, have stressed the theme of continuity in the development of settlement patterns since pre-Roman times. Dr. M. E. Witherick, in particular, has put forward the view that Cornwall's earliest towns were the result of native economic and social forces, which saw the gradual transformation over several centuries of hamlet into village and village into town. To Witherick, the granting of a borough charter by some medieval dignitary only rarely represents the actual creation of a town but rather recognition of what had already become a reality.

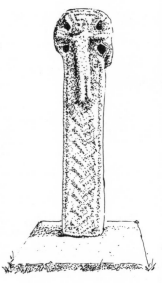

*A 10th-century standing cross*

At the heart of the problem, as we have seen, lies the paucity of documentary evidence as town records for Cornwall are very meagre before the 13th century. The Domesday Survey of 1086 is particularly uninformative although it says enough to suggest that a few communities were already regarded as towns; but we should remember that most early medieval towns would have contained only a few hundred inhabitants and would have looked to the modern eye more like overgrown country villages. The Survey recorded Bodmin as the largest town, but with only 68 houses, while the ecclesiastical settlement of St Stephen's-by-Launceston seems to have originated as a Saxon township. Interestingly, both examples illustrate how important was the presence of a monastery as a stimulus to early growth. Previous references

*Decorated font, Bodmin church*

51

to Domesday Book, though, have shown that it has its limitations, and other evidence suggests that communities like Padstow, Launceston itself, Kilkhampton and Helston were also assuming town characteristics and functions.

During the 12th century, town development accelerated with growth stimulated by economic forces and by the conferring of trading privileges. Authority to hold a regular weekly market was particularly coveted, a right granted to the men of East Looe by Henry II, while in 1194 Robert of Cardinham paid 10 marks to enjoy the same privilege at Lostwithiel. At some point between 1190 and 1225 Prior Theobald of Tywardreath established a free borough at Fowey which quickly grew into Cornwall's most important medieval port. Again, in or about 1173, Earl Reginald granted a charter of privileges 'to my free burgesses of Truro', a document interestingly addressed 'to the barons of Cornwall, and all men both Cornish and English'. During the 13th and 14th centuries this process accelerated, and by 1400 about thirty-five settlements enjoyed sufficient privileges and performed enough functions to warrant classification as towns. Some of them, like Callington, St Columb Major, St Ives and Wadebridge, did not enjoy the formal status of a borough but still had the lucrative right to hold weekly markets. These were exceptions, however, and most of the county's early towns were classified as boroughs either because they had been granted a charter or because they traditionally claimed such a status by prescription. Borough charters were coveted documents which conferred special privileges on the inhabitants and exempted them from normal judicial customary obligations. The basic criterion was the possession of free burgage tenure, which gave the burgess or tenant the right to hold his burgage or house plot without having to perform the kind of labour service expected from an ordinary villein. As well as being allowed to hold regular markets, boroughs could host annual fairs and assume responsibility for the administration of justice within their designated boundaries. As the Lostwithiel example showed, borough status was often worth paying for, and in 1201 the men of Helston paid 40 marks of silver to King John 'that their town be made a free borough with gild merchant'.

*Pengersick Castle: a fortified manor house*

With about thirty medieval boroughs Cornwall occupied an impressive third position in the national county hierarchy and was only surpassed by Somerset, with 31, and Devon with seventy-four. It is far from clear, however, exactly why the south-west in general had so many boroughs when the more fertile and populous counties of East Anglia and the Midlands had so few. For Cornwall the earldom was certainly a stimulus, and Earl Richard, in particular, granted charters to Bossiney, Tintagel, Camelford, West Looe, Bodmin, Launceston, Liskeard and Lostwithiel, although the last four, at least, were already established towns at the time of their incorporation. The increase in Cornwall's maritime importance must also have played a part, and the concentration of boroughs along the south coast including Looe,

52

Penzance, St Mawes and Penryn reflects the growing importance of trade to the county's economy. Others, though, seem to have been purely speculative ventures which hardly got off the ground, quickly reverting to country villages in the aftermath of the Black Death and in the fluctuating economic climate of the 15th century. Few today would imagine that tiny Crafthole near St Germans had been granted a charter in 1314 or that Mitchell and Tregony once enjoyed the same status as Bodmin and Penzance. Some foundations were even recognised as failures almost from the start, like the borough of Penknight which Earl Richard wisely amalgamated with nearby Lostwithiel in 1268.

Not only was the town map of medieval Cornwall very different from its modern counterpart but the urban hierarchy had an unfamiliar look to it. Population estimates for this period depend on the survival of burgess totals and, while many have been lost, it is still possible to reach a few generalisations. In the first place, several of today's largest towns were still in their infancy, overshadowed by communities which would now be classified as villages. In 1306, for example, Boscastle was a borough of 100 burgesses, perhaps 500 people in all, while 20 years later Penzance had a population of only about a hundred and fifty. Tintagel, with 86 burgesses, was bigger than East Looe and Camelford with about sixty each, while modern urban centres like St Austell were mere hamlets and Falmouth hardly existed at all before 1613. Those towns which occupied the very top of the urban ladder, on the other hand, were more familiar places which have managed to retain their importance through the centuries. Bodmin was particularly important, enjoying the advantages which stemmed from its geographical position in the centre of the county. Mentioned in Domesday Book, it was the religious centre of Cornwall throughout the Middle Ages; its Augustinian priory was reconstituted by Bishop Warlewast of Exeter between 1107–37, and it had a Franciscan friary and numerous chapels. The borough's importance was also enhanced by its early rôle as the most important tin market in the county. The second largest town was Truro which had been granted a borough charter in or about 1173. Thereafter it grew rapidly, being chosen as the home of the Sheriff's Tourn and by the end of the 1250s the borough also housed a Dominican friary. In addition the burgesses enjoyed the familiar right to hold a weekly market together with an annual fair in November, and the town's importance was further recognised in 1295 when along with Bodmin, Tregony, Launceston and Liskeard it was allowed to send two representatives to Edward I's Parliament, a privilege which it continued to exercise right up to the Second Reform Act of 1867. As the tin industry expanded and continued in its westward advance Truro also became a coinage town, as did Cornwall's third largest medieval borough, Lostwithiel. This community expanded under the patronage of the Cardinham family (originally known as Cardinan), although its precise origins are lost in the mists of the 12th century. In or about 1195 Robert *de Cardinan* granted his burgesses of *Lostwetell*

*St Petrock's chest, Bodmin*

53

'all the liberties which his ancestors had given them', adding the frustratingly uninformative comment 'on the day when they were founded'. Each burgess was to rent his burgage at the rate of 6d. a year, half the normal requirement. In 1268 Lostwithiel was amalgamated with adjoining Penknight, granted a market, fair, gild merchant and other privileges, and by the early 14th century it had become a leading coinage town as well as the headquarters of the Duchy administration. From a burgage total of 305 recorded in 1300 the number of houseplots had risen to 400 by 1337, which suggests a total population of between one and two thousand. Helston, Liskeard, Fowey and Launceston were also important Cornish towns throughout the medieval period, the first two as coinage towns, Fowey as a thriving maritime centre. Launceston, with its important castle enlarged by Earl Richard, was a major administrative and judicial centre and interestingly it was the only Cornish town to be surrounded and defended by stone walls and gates. In places the walls were six ft. thick and substantial in height as they were raised on the top of a large earthen bank, but centuries of robbing for house-building have left only the Southgate remaining.

*A bench-end carving from St Ives church*

For the inhabitants of these early towns life varied considerably according to the economic pursuits of the immediate locality. It was usual for the burgesses to have their strips or 'stitches' in the common fields which can still be detected around Penryn, Marazion, Bossiney and elsewhere. Some towns, as we have seen, benefited from the expansion of the tin industry and were designated coinage towns where the ore was weighed and taxed. The boroughs of St Germans, fostered by the wealthy Arundell family, and Lostwithiel were renowned for their pottery while the inhabitants of Boscastle, Looe, Mousehole, Padstow, Penryn, Penzance, St Ives and St Mawes were heavily involved in the fishing industry. Maritime functions, in fact, developed an increasing importance as the Middle Ages progressed and as Cornwall became steadily assimilated into the medieval trading orbit. Despite the many fluctuations in output, tin was the county's staple export, though the expansion of the cloth industry proved a boon to the burgesses of Fowey who handled most of the trade. During the first half of the 15th century, in fact, exports of cloth from Cornish ports increased 10-fold and these kinds of trading activity help us to account for another characteristic of the early town – the large numbers of foreigners recorded in contemporary tax returns. Many native Cornishmen do not seem to have been particularly attracted to urban life at this time and the vacuum was often filled with outsiders, with the result that many early towns, especially those on the coast, became quite cosmopolitan in their population. Evidence for this is derived from the Subsidy Rolls which conveniently separated native taxpayers from foreign ones, most of whom clearly came from similar maritime regions on the Continent. In 1327 there were 15 foreigners at Fowey; in the same year Penryn was equally divided between natives and foreigners and at Tregony and Grampound the foreign element actually predominated. By 1437 almost

54

one-third of the population of Fowey was classified as 'alien' and the great majority came from Ireland and Holland with a scattering also of Flemish and French inhabitants. Cornwall's traditional association with Brittany also continued to be reflected in similar fashion and again most of the county's ports contained a sizeable Breton minority. Fowey again headed the list; a later subsidy roll of Henry VIII recorded the presence of 23 foreigners at St Ives, all Bretons, while the surrounding parishes also housed a liberal sprinkling of Breton families. It is clear, in fact, that up to the Reformation Bretons were still coming to Cornwall in impressive numbers and when war broke out between England and France in the 1540s we hear of the dilemma faced by many who 'would rather die than go hence'. The conflict prompted many to become naturalised and it is noticeable in the later subsidy rolls that while the number of Bretons listed as foreigners decreases, the surname 'Briton' or 'Brette' becomes more common. Other Breton names entered the local nomenclature and in the Penwith area, in particular, surnames like Jewell, Tangye, Gruzelier and Rouffignac'h still survive as evidence of this long-standing connection between Cornwall and 'little Britain'.

*Roche hermitage*

Some of the early towns already discussed have shown the importance of a monastic community in providing a stimulus to urban development. A resident community of monks often enjoyed the privilege of holding a regular market which in turn attracted traders and craftsmen quick to appreciate the advantages of a permanent site. The Augustinians were the principal order in Cornwall with priories at Bodmin, Tregony, St Germans and Launceston, and their foundations clearly acted as strong nucleating forces, just as another priory at St Anthony-in-Roseland may have been a factor in the growth of nearby St Mawes. In addition there were important collegiate churches at St Columb Major and at Penryn, where Glasney College emerged as a centre of Cornish literary activity; most medieval towns, in fact, had their stock of churches, chapels and related institutions which stimulated economic and urban growth. By 1400 the borough of Penryn housed the chapels of SS Mary and Leonard, a bishop's palace, a chantry, as well as the once magnificent Glasney collegiate church begun by Bishop Brones-combe of Exeter in 1264. Demolished during the Reformation, this fortified residence for 26 clerics had its church, domestic quarters, refectory, chapter-house and its own cemetery. The borough of Truro, later to become a cathedral city, was already an established religious centre with its Dominican friary and three chapels dedicated to SS Mary, George and Nicholas, while the spiritual needs of the people of Padstow were so well catered for that the vicar in 1745 lamented that 'there were seven or eight chapels in my parish but they are all in ruins and the names of most are entirely forgotten'.

An essential part of the duties of the medieval church, at least since the Fourth Lateran Council of 1215, involved catering for the sick, aged and infirm, and for pilgrims en route to one of Cornwall's many

55

*St Michael's Mount:*
*place of pilgrimage*

holy shrines like St Michael's Mount. Several towns had their hospices for this purpose, like St John's Hospice at Helston; the 'Lazar House' for lepers was also a common feature of the Cornish landscape. Leprosy was a frequent ailment in the Middle Ages, and in 1179 the Church ordered the Christian community everywhere to show a more benevolent attitude towards sufferers. By 1309 two lazar houses at Bodmin were catering for 39 lepers, and there were others at St Ives, Truro, Helston and Padstow. Often, though, mistaken fear of contamination prompted other leper houses to be built well away from centres of population, and the Cornish word *clodgy* or *clojy* (meaning 'sick house') can be found in several remote locations. In his will, Bishop Bytton of Exeter (1291–1307) left legacies to as many as 23 leper hospices in the county, stating that the money was to be apportioned 'to every sick person — twelve pence'.

In the countryside as well as in the towns the Church was an essential ingredient of medieval life. In general, though, it was not rural monasticism which made a significant contribution to Cornish society, although the communities at Tywardreath and St Buryan were important, but the numerous local churches which were the mainstay of Christian worship. As we have seen in Chapter Four many of these churches had their roots in the sixth and seventh centuries when Celtic Christianity was at its height, but only about one third, just over two hundred, seem to have been selected as parish churches. It is not really clear when the parochial system was first introduced into the county, though it seems reasonable to assume that the process began with the Anglo-Saxons in the eastern area and was completed by the first generation of Normans. Certainly by the early 12th century the pattern had become clear, and parish boundaries often coincided with manorial limits which in turn appear to represent much older territorial divisions. At all events, the 12th century saw an energetic phase of church building, although relatively little architectural evidence from this period has survived the later programmes of rebuilding and expansion. Tintagel church, however, remains as a fine example of the late Norman style with its familiar cruciform shape and north and south transepts. Each parish church was attached to one of Cornwall's eight deaneries, whose borders closely corresponded to those of the hundreds, while the archdeacon exercised authority on behalf of the Bishop of Exeter.

During the late Middle Ages the Church fell into general disrepute for a number of inter-related reasons. The tithe was particularly resented and the resentment was aggravated by the increasing trend towards appropriation, by which the revenue of a parish was often diverted to a monastery, frequently beyond the county. By the late 15th century over half the Cornish parishes had been appropriated and this was condemned by those who paid the tithe but saw little in return. The moral and spiritual standards of the clergy had also declined, and not without reason did Bishop Grandisson refer to them as 'corrupters

*A female leper: a*
*common sight in*
*medieval Cornwall*

56

rather than leaders . . . riotous and debauched'. There were numerous complaints about the behaviour of individual clerics for neglect of duty, ignorance of the scriptures and moral lapses, while many benefices were neglected as priests took on several parishes to increase their incomes and then failed to provide an adequate service to their enlarged flock. Monastic life also deteriorated with allegations of ignorance and sexual debauchery, and at St Germans in 1355 only four of the 10 canons could even write their own names. When Edward IV appointed a commission to reform the important collegiate church at St Buryan, it was found that the dean and prebendaries lived elsewhere, the curates led a life of drunkenness and fornication, and the church's fabric was decaying at a faster rate than the morality of the inmates. Half a century later Henry VIII was to address himself to the fundamental issue of the Church's status, although he could never have envisaged the reaction his measures were to provoke among the Cornish people themselves.

*The decadent clergy: a medieval depiction of an inebriated monk*

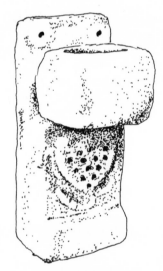

*A 15h-century holy water stoup from Egloshayle*

# VII Cornwall and the Tudors: Rebellions and Reformation

*The 15 bezants of Cornwall*

'Up to the 16th century, Cornwall was the last outpost of the known world.' So wrote the county's most famous historian, A. L. Rowse, in his authoritative study *Tudor Cornwall*, first published in 1941. A century of conflict with France and Spain, however, punctuated by the Reformation and no less than three rebellions, was to end this isolation and bring Cornwall firmly into the mainstream of British national life.

It may well have been this remoteness which saved the county from the dynastic squabbles of the Wars of the Roses which brought confusion to so much of the country during the late 15th century. While others aligned themselves with either the White Rose of York or the Red Rose of Lancaster, the two branches of the Plantagenets competing for the throne of England, the Cornish showed only a passing interest. The sympathies of the people, though, were basically Lancastrian, and several leading Cornish families like the Courtenays played an active part elsewhere, only to pay a heavy price for opposing Yorkists through the execution of three of their leading members. Others, like Sir Henry de Bodrugan, were obliged to forfeit their lands and flee the country as their price for 'backing the wrong horse'. In contrast, supporters of Henry Tudor were generously rewarded after his victory at Bosworth in 1485; the Treffrys of Fowey received several important manors forfeited by Yorkist sympathisers while the Lancastrian loyalist Sir Richard Edgecumbe was elevated to the Privy Council and went on to become a trusted member of the new king's court. For the ordinary people, on the other hand, more interested in the coming harvest or when the next shoal of pilchards might appear, these must have been strange goings on with little relevance to their everyday lives. What was of interest, though, was how much taxation the new Henry VII might try to exact from them and what action could they take to avoid paying it. Few in 1485 would have anticipated the scale of resentment which was to erupt 12 years later.

In 1497 the Cornish exploded onto the national stage with two uprisings against the Crown. The people had a long tradition of independence which stemmed from racial identity, geographical remoteness and centuries of relative isolation; in 1342 the retiring Archdeacon of Cornwall, Adam de Carlton, had observed that 'the folk of these parts are quite extraordinary, being of a rebellious temper, and obdurate in the face of attempts to teach and correct'. The tinners had a particularly

*Cotehele, a late 15th-century manor house*

notorious reputation; a century and a half later they could still be regarded as 'twelve thousand of the roughest and most mutinous men in England'. This underlying distaste for authority was now to be brought to the surface by the king's attempts to raise funds for a campaign against James IV of Scotland. In January 1497 Parliament approved a new round of taxation which was likely to affect the poorer classes as well as the gentry.

Four Royal Commissioners were appointed to assess the tax in Cornwall, John Arundell, John Trevenor, Thomas Erisey and Richard Flamank, but almost immediately unrest began to surface among the people of the Lizard who, like the tinners, were renowned for their fierce independence. They quickly rallied around the leadership of a St Keverne blacksmith, Michael Joseph *Angof* ('the smith'), and the dissent soon spread throughout Cornwall. Support came from all sections of society and all parts of the county as the rebels marched across the Tamar and on to London. By now they had been joined by a Bodmin lawyer, Thomas Flamank, ironically the son of one of the tax assessors, while in Somerset they gained their most prominent recruit, Lord James Audley. It appears that the rebels had hoped to gain the support of the men of Kent who were also known for their rebellious nature but this was not forthcoming and seriously weakened their chances of success. The king, meanwhile, had been caught by surprise but was fortunate in that his newly-assembled Scottish army had not yet been sent north and so its commander, Lord Daubeney, was first ordered to disperse the Cornishmen. By Friday 16 June the rebels, said to have been 15,000 strong, had reached the outskirts of London and had set up camp on Blackheath. The royal forces, however, had been swollen to 25,000 and the outcome of the confrontation was inevitable. On the following day the rebels were surrounded, and 'being ill-armed and ill-lead [*sic*], and without horse or artillery, they were with no great difficulty cut in pieces and put to flight' (Francis Bacon). About 200 were apparently killed and the leaders, Arundell, Flamank and Angof, were sentenced to death, Angof going to the gallows in a blaze of defiance claiming that 'he should have a name perpetual, and a fame permanent and immortal'. Posterity, in fact, came rather belatedly for the blacksmith and it was not until 1966 that a memorial to him was finally erected in the churchyard of his native St Keverne. The remainder of the rebels were allowed to drift despondently homewards, the king having been persuaded against any large-scale reprisals for fear of provoking further unrest. This was sound advice for, as one contemporary noted, the Cornish had been 'little mollified or quieted, and were ready to move again and begin new commotions and conspiracies'.

Henry VII may well have resented his leniency, for within weeks the Cornishmen were taking up arms against him for the second time. They now threw their lot behind Perkin Warbeck, a Flemish imposter who professed to be Richard, Duke of York, one of the Princes of the Tower and as such a claimant to the throne. Warbeck had landed at Whitsand

*Perkin Warbeck, the 1497 imposter*

Bay near Sennen on 7 September with a force of about 200 from Ireland. His intention was to recruit an army from the disgruntled thousands who had wound their weary way back from Blackheath, and within days 3,000 had joined him at Bodmin where he now proclaimed himself to be Richard IV. Warbeck's plan was to take Exeter, and by 17 September the rebels, by then 6,000 strong, had assembled at the city gates but, after briefly breaching the walls, they were pushed back and forced to retreat. In the meantime royal reinforcements, again led by Daubeney and aided by Sir Rhys ap Thomas, had arrived on the scene and their presence was enough to dishearten the rebels who began to drift away. On the night of 21 September the imposter himself deserted those who remained, only to be captured on 5 October and held at Exeter. One observer noted that 'it was necessary to guard him well, in order that the men of Cornwall may not murder him, as they are incensed since they have learned from the King that they have been worshipping a low born foreigner as their sovereign'. In the end Henry VII did the job for them; Warbeck was taken back to London and the Tower, given enough room to attempt an abortive escape and then hanged.

As with the aftermath of the first rebellion the king did not follow a policy of widespread recriminations, although a few of the ringleaders were again executed. As Professor Bindoff wrote, however, 'the West Country kept its gallows empty at the cost of emptying its pockets'; substantial fines were imposed on the Cornish people for years to come and the county paid heavily for its independent spirit. Cornwall's relative isolation from the centre of national life had also been abruptly shattered and the process of absorption was to accelerate during the next century as the Reformation, another uprising, and a succession of wars with France and Spain brought this remote corner of Britain firmly into the orbit of English and European affairs.

War had broken out with France in 1511 and west-country ports immediately came under the threat of naval attack. In reality this hardly materialised, although in 1514 the little borough of Marazion near Penzance was burnt in a raid, and a map compiled shortly afterwards showed much of the town in ruins. It was only to be in the aftermath of Henry VIII's confrontation with the Papacy that the Cornish coast was to be seriously threatened by the might of Catholic France and Spain. In 1534 Parliament passed the Act of Succession sanctioning the annulment of the king's marriage to Catherine of Aragon and declaring the succession to the throne vested in the children of Henry's second marriage to Anne Boleyn. This was followed by an Act of Supremacy and in 1536 by the Dissolution of the smaller monasteries.

A campaign against the increasingly irrelevant and unholy monasteries had been imminent for some time and became almost inevitable with the appointment of Thomas Cromwell as Vicar-General. Logically the Cornish should have welcomed this development; a survey of 1535

*A satire on the greed of monks*

60

had valued the Cornish monasteries at £4,083 but most of this income was spent well beyond the Tamar. The revenues came mainly from rents and the unpopular tithes, like the 1/18th of their catch which the fishermen of Golant had to pay to the prior of Tywardreath. By 1536 the dissolution of the larger religious houses was also well on the way but not without some plaintive pleas for special treatment; the prior of Bodmin wrote optimistically to Cromwell 'trusting you will continue my good lord, as ye have ever done, and remember me and my poor brethren to the king's commissioners at their coming into Cornwall for our poor living'. The head of Cornwall's largest priory and favourite destination for pilgrims anxious to see the relics of St Petroc had little grounds for pleading poverty, but his letter may not have been in vain; he received an annual pension of £66 13s. 4d. while the canons were only awarded £5 6s. 8d. The prior of Launceston, though, apparently without any pleading, received the fairly handsome pension of £100, and on the whole the brothers were well taken care of. So also were the king's agents who supervised the dissolution process, like Dr. Tregonwell who accumulated considerable wealth plus an annual pension of £40.

After the Dissolution most of the church lands eventually passed into the hands of lay landholders, which considerably strengthened the economic position of the Cornish gentry and helped to create the kind of semi-aristocratic class largely absent from Cornish life to date. Bodmin priory, for example, was sold to Thomas Sternhold in 1544, St Germans was leased to John Champernowne for under £7 a year, while the Prideaux family did well out of the Padstow estates. From the Crown's standpoint, the process not only produced much needed revenue, but created a body of dependant subjects whose loyalty was to be needed in the face of Counter-Reformation sentiment and increasing threats from continental Catholic powers. Spanish and French raiders had already penetrated the Fal estuary, prompting Henry VIII to order the construction of castles at Pendennis and St Mawes in 1539 and another, St Catherine's, at Fowey a year later. The problem was cost, for the process of creating a network of Channel defences was proving expensive and, although peace came temporarily in 1546, excessive taxation only added fuel to the embers of discontent among the ordinary Cornish people who viewed all changes, including religious, with profound scepticism and distaste.

*Pendennis Castle*

The anticipated threat to the new religion was in fact to come from home, not abroad. The government had been concerned about the staunchly Catholic south-west for some time and had taken the precaution in 1539 of setting up a Council of the West to enforce the changes and to deal with any possible disturbances. Matters came to a head in January 1549 after Parliament passed the Act of Uniformity by which English was to replace Latin in all church services from 9 June onwards. For a simple, traditional people this was all too much and in no time the county was again in a state of uproar. Penryn, in particular,

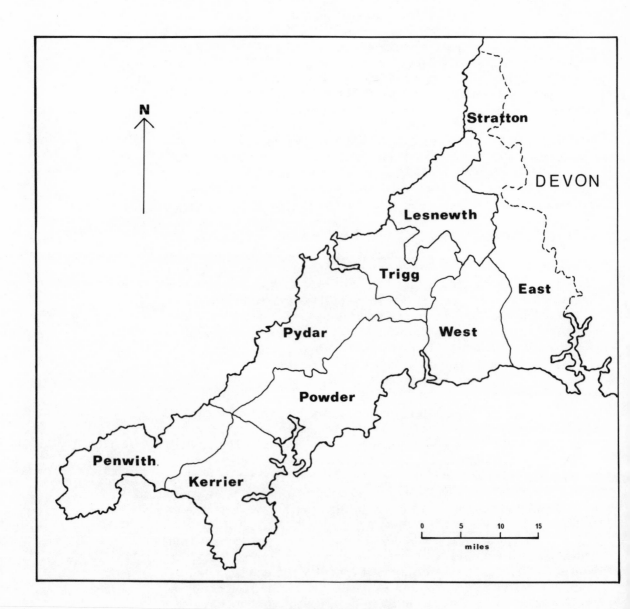

The Cornish hundreds.

62

quickly emerged as a hotbed of dissent while rebels from Penwith attacked St Michael's Mount and laid waste to nearby Marazion causing 'great decay, ruin and desolation'. Humphry Arundell of Helland emerged as the main leader of what was to be dubbed the 'Prayer Book Rebellion' and the insurgents proceeded to Bodmin where they were joined by the mayor, Nicholas Boyer.

It was there that they drew up their staunchly conservative petition to the king, saying 'we will not receyve the new servyce because it is but lyke a Christmas game, but we wyll have our olde service of mattens, Masse, evensong and procession in Latten as it was before, and so we Cornysshe men, where of certen of us understand no English, utterly refuse thys newe Englysh'. Even fewer, of course, would have understood Latin either but the familiarity of the traditional service and usages was the cherished issue at stake. Inevitably, their demands were rejected and the rebels, now 2,000 strong, marched to Exeter and surrounded the city on 2 July. At the end of the month, though, the siege was partially lifted and a large contingent of rebels proceeded to Honiton only to be defeated by a royal force under Lord Grey. Far from abandoning their cause, however, the Cornish staged a rearguard action at Sampford Courtenay but all to no avail. The leaders were executed and many priests sympathetic to the rebellion were deprived of their livings while some, like the curate of Pillaton, were publicly executed. Other lay leaders suffered the confiscation of their property on the orders of Lord Russell, overall commander of the royal forces, who was duly rewarded with the earldom of Bedford for his troubles. The wrath of the authorities was also felt in a less predictable manner; all church bells save the smallest in each tower were ordered to be taken down, although fortunately for posterity the directive was not enforced and only the bell clappers were actually removed. For the moment, at least, the Cornish could no longer be summoned by chimes into rebellion.

After the 1549 uprising Protestantism proceeded at full speed, altars were removed, a second Prayer Book issued in 1542 and another Act of Uniformity passed to enforce it. All this had considerable effect on the course of Cornish history; the intimate connection with Catholic Brittany was severed, while the absence of a Cornish translation of the new service accelerated the decline of the language which lost substantial ground throughout the following century. Literature in Cornish also suffered with the suppression of Glasney college at Penryn which had been an important cultural bastion of the old language. While Catholicism was subsequently restored under Queen Mary in 1553, her brief five-year reign was not enough to ensure any lasting reversals and the lengthy rule of her successor Elizabeth I saw to it that the old Catholic days were gone for good. This is not to say, of course, that individual adherance to the old faith did not continue and for some of these recusants, as they were now styled, life proved to be difficult and, for a minority, impossible. The staunchly Catholic Arundells of

*Slate memorial from Lanivet church*

63

Lanherne rejected the new religion, and in 1584 Sir John Arundell was despatched to the Tower where he died six years later. Another recusant, Cuthbert Mayne, was hanged in the market place at Launceston, dismembered, and then his still quivering heart was cut out and held up to the assembled masses. If that was not enough, his severed head was displayed on the castle gate and quarters of his body sent to four other towns for display as a lesson to others. Even for those fortunate enough to avoid prison and keep their heads, the payment of annual fines for recusancy kept them impoverished for decades to come. At the village level, however, it would be wrong to exaggerate the immediate effects of the Reformation in Cornwall and some of the religious changes were slow to permeate local life. Many Catholic practices continued to be observed; and in 1584 the vicar of Kilkhampton claimed not even to know that a new Prayer Book existed, and Mass was still being celebrated in some parish churches as late as 1590. Deprived of local leaders and spiritual direction, though, the old faith steadily faded away and by the end of the century the Church of England in Cornwall had gained a firm hold.

In 1584, after a long period of deteriorating relations, war had broken out with Catholic Spain. The vulnerability of the south-west prompted extra provision to be made for coastal defence, and Sir Francis Godolphin and Sir William Mohun were appointed deputy-lieutenants to make the necessary preparations for King Philip's anticipated invasion. Ordnance was sent down to St Michael's Mount and a force of 5,000 assembled in readiness. At Plymouth, meanwhile, Francis Drake gathered a fleet to defend the western approaches, and after several false alarms the Spanish Armada of 130 ships was finally spotted off the Lizard on 7 July 1588. Its defeat and subsequent flight entered the folklore of English history, but few believed that Spanish pride and determination would be satisfied without a second attempt. The next decade, in fact, was dominated by rumours of further armadas, and even more defensive work along the south-western coastline was required, including the fortification of the Isles of Scilly. Eventually, on 23 July 1595, a small force of 200 Spaniards landed in Mount's Bay at Mousehole and proceeded to fulfil an old Cornish prophecy that strangers would one day 'burn Paul, Penzance and Newlyn'. After this early success, however, the intruders eventually fled at the sight of English men-of-war despatched by Drake from Plymouth, and Spanish attention was fortunately diverted towards supporting the Irish in their latest rebellion against the Crown. At long last the threat of attack on Cornwall was lifted and the accession of James I in 1603 finally brought peace and respite not only from war but from the heavy burden of taxation which had accompanied it.

During these decades of unrest and external threats Cornish society and economic life had still managed to develop. The three principal industries of agriculture, tin and fishing all experienced steady growth characterised by the introduction of new ideas and technology. The

*A Spanish galleon*

29. (*above*) Silver and brass bands have long been a feature of Cornish life, particularly in the old mining areas. This example of *c.* 1895 is from Veryan, near Truro.

30. (*below*) Three elderly Cornish ladies in deep discussion, with best china and Sunday bonnets.

31.  The Cunard liner *Malta* run ashore in fog in 1889, with Botallack Head in the background.

32.  The tanker *Torrey Canyon* wrecked on the Sevenstones Reef in 1967. Her 119,000 tons of crude oil caused widespread pollution.

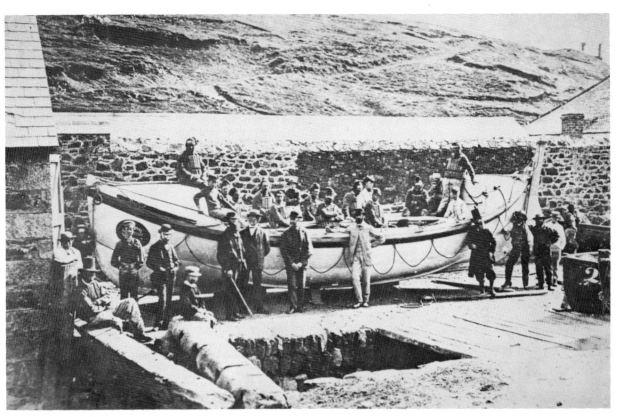

33. (*above*) The Mullion lifeboat, *Daniel J. Draper*, with crew and villagers outside its house in the cove, *c.* 1880.
34. (*below*) The little china clay port of Charlestown, St Austell, 1910.

35.  East front of Trerice.

36.  Place, Fowey.

fishing communities were transformed by the advent of seine fishing, which saw the formation of local syndicates owning several boats which shared a single large net. This innovation brought about a marked increase in catches and in the export of pilchards, or *fumadoes* as they were known locally, to Ireland and the Mediterranean. Throughout the whole of the Tudor period tin ranked alongside wool and lead as a major national export and in Cornwall the development of the industry accelerated through the enterprise of local landholders such as the Godolphins, whose speculations created great personal wealth. The 16th century saw the transition from tin-streaming to mining proper, with the necessary expertise imported in the shape of German engineers renowned for their technical superiority. Copper was also becoming an increasingly important commodity, and close links were forged with South Wales where the ore was sent for smelting. In the past, periods of mining expansion had often proved detrimental to farming since, as Richard Carew put it in his famous *Survey Of Cornwall* of 1602, 'the Cornish people gave themselves principally, and in a manner wholly, to the seeking of tin and neglected husbandry'. This was not to be the case now, however, for agriculture experienced a general improvement during the late 16th century, and Carew points out that wheat was the main crop with rye grown on the poorer soils, although barley was becoming increasingly popular everywhere. He also adds the qualification that West Cornwall was generally less advanced than the East where profits were higher and the demand for land much more intense.

*Master mariner, Sir Richard Grenville*

This expansion of the economy and the rise in exports stimulated the growth of the Cornish merchant fleet which had reached 68 ships by 1582. The general increase in wealth also produced a corresponding increase in the number of continental vessels visiting Cornish ports with their cargoes of linen, cloths, salt and wine destined for the tables of the prospering gentry who, like the Edgecumbes at Cotehele, the Arundells at Trerice and the Killigrews at Arwenack, were channelling their wealth into new and impressive manor houses. The expansion of the economy also contributed to a new phase of urban growth which was reflected in the large number of charters granted to Cornish towns and in the substantial increase in borough representation in Parliament. By 1584 no less than 21 communities had been elevated to the status of two-member boroughs which meant that the county, also with its standard quota of two shire members, sent no less than 44 M.P.s to London, only one less than the whole of Scotland! While the largest town, Bodmin with about 2,000 inhabitants, clearly warranted separate representation, many of the other parliamentary boroughs, like Mitchell and St Mawes, were mere villages with no such justifiable claim. Perhaps the increasing importance of Cornwall's ports, reflected during the previous continental wars, as well as the growth in commerce, were the factors behind this clearly excessive spate of incorporation.

Beyond the towns, work and leisure among the country folk were both becoming more diverse. The expansion of mining and fishing widened the county's economic base and enabled farmers and their labourers to diversify their interests and lessen their dependence on a single enterprise. Carew noted that all this was reflected in improvements to the housing stock with the introduction of plaster and glass, and he gives an overall impression that the standard of living for all classes was steadily advancing. His *Survey* provides a fascinating insight, too, into the rural culture of 16th-century Cornwall, with comments on the state of the language as well as detailed descriptions of sports and local customs. A major annual event was the local feast day when parish saints were revered in an atmosphere of general revelry which also accompanied the midsummer eve bonfires lit along the length and breadth of the county. The distinctive local version of Celtic wrestling was also popular, and the Cornish were noted too for their skill in archery, a characteristic which they shared with the Welsh. The game of hurling, or 'soule' as it was then known, was widely played, though often chaotically, as the sport involved teams of up to forty a side whose object was to reach a fixed destination with a large wooden ball in an atmosphere of frenzied excitement in which virtually anything appears to have been allowed. On a more sedate level, Carew also noted the Cornish attachment to miracle plays which attracted 'country people from all sides, many miles off, to hear and see it, for they have therein devils and devices to delight as well the eye as the ear'. These plays combined religion with a populist tone and the performances were great open-air events, often held over several days, with side shows and other entertainers adding variety to the occasion. Special amphitheatres were built for the purpose, and several of these *plen-an-gwary* or 'playing places' still remain, like the one in the centre of St Just. The most important of the miracle plays was the 15th-century trilogy the *Ordinalia*, although others have survived, including *Gwyreans an Bys* ('the Creation of the World') and *Beunans Meriasek* ('Life of St Meriasek'). As the titles suggest, these plays were performed in Cornish, although the texts which have come down to us reflect the increasing use of English loan-words at a time when the native language was rapidly beginning to lose ground. While many factors contributed to the irreversible decline of Cornish, the upheaval and dislocation caused by Charles I's clash with Parliament and the Civil War which followed played an important part.

# VIII  The Seventeenth Century: Civil War and Restoration

Cornwall played a significant rôle in the constitutional squabbles of the 17th century, when the issue of 'King or Parliament' divided the nation to such a degree that it took a civil war to resolve it. The county, after all, sent 44 M.P.s to Parliament, or 39 more than today, and so it enjoyed a political influence out of all proportion to its size and population. As it transpired, the allegiance of the Cornish was to lie with the Crown, but this was far from obvious during the early years of Charles I's reign when discontent manifested itself in 1626 over the Forced Loan, when the hard-pressed inhabitants were obliged to provide £2,000 for the king. Prominent among national figures opposed both to the level of early Stuart taxation and to the influence of the royal favourite, the Duke of Buckingham, was the Cornishman Sir John Eliot who was accordingly despatched to the Tower where he died in November 1632. His death fuelled the dissident temperament of a people who had already shown themselves to be no respecters of authority. The mood was strengthened as a result of the economic dislocation caused by Turkish pirates in the Channel, about whom the Crown appeared to be doing very little. When the famous Long Parliament met in 1640 Cornish members shared the rising Puritan sentiment of the day and their frustration over the king's reluctance to recognise the power of Parliament was aggravated by yet more taxation and especially the unpopular poll tax. When, during the early months of 1642, the possibility of compromise vanished, however, deep-rooted monarchist sentiment, natural conservatism, and a complex web of family ties and traditions prevented many from deserting Charles when he raised his standard at Nottingham in August. Leading families like the Arundells, Vyvyans, Godolphins and Killigrews rallied to his cause and overshadowed the Cornish Parliamentarians, who included in their ranks Lord Robartes of Lanhydrock, Edmund Prideaux and John St Aubyn. Smaller men, in turn, tended to follow their gentry landlords, and within a few weeks the county had divided into opposing camps, anxiously awaiting news of national developments.

At the end of September a Royalist force under the command of Sir Ralph Hopton crossed the Tamar and proceeded to recruit additional supporters. By the end of the following month Launceston castle had been taken for the king and Hopton had secured control of virtually the whole county. Most of the leading Parliamentarians had fled to Plymouth, a stronghold of their cause, and were encouraged by news

*A late 17th-century silver cup from Launceston*

67

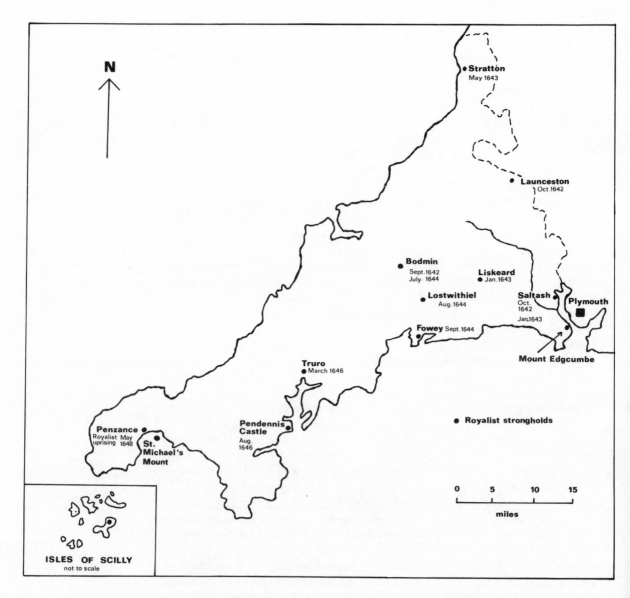

N

● Stratton
May 1643

● Launceston
Oct.1642

● Bodmin
Sept.1642
July· 1644

● Liskeard
● Jan.1643

● Lostwithiel
Aug.1644

Saltash ●
Oct.
1642
Jan.1643

■ Plymouth

● Fowey Sept.1644

Mount Edgcumbe

● Truro
● March 1646

● Royalist strongholds

Penzance ●
Royalist May
uprising 1648

St.
Michael's
Mount

Pendennis
Castle
●
Aug.
1646

0      5      10      15

miles

ISLES OF SCILLY
not to scale

The Civil War in Cornwall, showing the main Royalist centres and dates of principal engagements.

that a Parliamentarian force under Colonel Ruthin had reached Cornwall. Any sense of relief proved short-lived, however, when Ruthin's army was routed at Liskeard in January 1643 and 1,250 prisoners were taken. A second defeat followed at Saltash, and Plymouth itself was now put under siege, although on 23 April another Parliamentary force, this time led by General James Chudleigh, crossed Poulston Bridge and marched on Launceston. After a long battle in which the advantage continually changed hands, Chudleigh was forced to order a general retreat and another and more decisive Royalist victory at Stratton effectively ended the war in Cornwall, though not the rôle of the Cornish in the wider conflict. At the end of July the country's second city, Bristol, fell to the king's supporters, but Cornish losses in the fighting were so severe, particularly among the leaders, that a separate Cornish army now ceased to exist and its remnants were drafted into other units. The death of the popular Royalist commander Sir Bevil Grenville, 'the most generally loved man in Cornwall', according to Clarendon, at the battle of Lansdown had been a particularly bitter blow. At home, meanwhile, life began to revert to normal, although committed Parliament men like Lord Robartes and Nicholas Boscawen had their estates confiscated by the loyalist sheriff, Francis Bassett, who was also left with the onerous burden of raising revenue for the king's cause as well as meeting the cost of defending the coast and paying for the new gun platforms on St Michael's Mount.

In the spring of the following year, however, the tide again turned and the Royalists began to experience a succession of reverses in the west. The 1644 campaigns are well documented, and the graphic accounts of contemporary diarists provide a full record of the main events. In July a Parliamentarian force under the Earl of Essex crossed the Tamar and took Bodmin, while at Lostwithiel they desecrated St Bartholomew's church and gutted the range of administrative buildings known as the 'Duchy Parliament'. The king was not slow to retaliate, and his loyal servant Sir Richard Grenville was ordered to raise a force and take action. Essex and his men were warned that 'they were entering a county exceedingly affectionate to His Majesty', and by August his force of 7,000 had become surrounded outside Fowey. Disaster, though, nearly hit the king on the 17th when a bullet fired at him while he was viewing the town from across the river narrowly missed, killing 'a poor fisherman' instead. The Parliamentarian cavalry, meanwhile, under the command of Sir William Balfour, attempted to break through the king's line but were defeated on the 31st, and Essex ignominiously escaped in a fishing boat to Plymouth. The survivors duly surrendered, and Charles turned his attention to the possibility of a full-scale attack on the city which stubbornly held out for Parliament under the charge of Lord Robartes of Lanhydrock. After much thought, though, this was considered foolhardy, and it was decided to concentrate on a policy of blockade which left Plymouth as an enclave of opposition and a focal point for future resistance. It

*The Earl of Essex*

69

*King Charles's Castle, Tresco*

may, in fact, have been just as well that the town was not in a stronger position for a contemporary noted that its inhabitants were 'eager to be avenged on the cursed Cornish who are as very heathen as the ignorant Welsh'.

In March 1645 Charles I sent his eldest son, the Prince of Wales, into the west as leader of the royal forces, but on a national level the tide was turning against the Crown. Determined to add a professional touch to their fighting the Parliamentarians had formed the New Model Army, and throughout July Fairfax and his troops advanced steadily westwards, seizing a vital Royalist arsenal at Bridgwater which included 44 barrels of gunpowder, and at the same time striking an important psychological blow. The surrender of Bristol on 10 September dealt the king's cause a crushing blow and, with Exeter also threatened, Sir Richard Grenville wrote that 'His Majesty hath no entire county in obedience but poor Cornwall'. Cornwall, though, was exhausted by a succession of financial levies and a continuous drain on manpower, and the hopelessness of the Royalist cause was further underlined when an extra 3,000 Parliamentarian recruits arrived at Totnes on 24 January. By 2 March Fairfax was at Bodmin and the Prince of Wales and his retinue were forced to flee, first to the Scillies and then to Jersey. On the mainland, meanwhile, the Royalist forces began to disintegrate despite the unswerving loyalty of Sir Ralph Hopton, but even he was forced to recognise the inevitable and surrendered on 12 March. Sir John Arundell held out in Pendennis Castle until August but his was a last defiant gesture among a people who had grown weary of war.

For the next 14 years the rule of Parliament was administered in Cornwall by the County Committee, which took on a wide range of responsibilities including the confiscation of the estates of the Royalist 'malignants'. Fighting briefly broke out again in May 1648 when Royalist rebels rose up at Penzance and Helston but after about seventy were killed they were soon beaten and their towns, we are told, were then 'exquisitely plundered' by Roundhead troops. The execution of Charles I on 30 January 1649 finally broke the resistance of the Cornish and in May 1651 the last Royalist outpost, the Isles of Scilly, were captured from Sir John Grenville by Admiral Blake.

On 16 December 1653 Oliver Cromwell was installed as Lord Protector and arrangements were made to elect a new Parliament in which Cornwall's representation was reduced, temporarily as it turned out, from 44 members to twelve. Royalists, in the meantime, continued to hope that the exiled Charles II would regain the throne and in 1654 the 'Sealed Knot' was formed to co-ordinate Cavalier activities and make preparations for a future uprising. Cornwall's representative was Grenville but the government was wise to his leanings and influence, and took the precaution of locking him up in Plymouth gaol. At the end of 1655 the country was put under the control of the military and Major-General John Desborough was made responsible for the six western counties. This proved to be an unpopular move and only served

*Hugh Peters of Fowey who helped send Charles I to the executioner's axe*

70

to fuel Royalist sentiment, which received a mighty boost in September 1658 with the death of Cromwell. Throughout the following year the possibility of restoring the monarchy became increasingly advocated as national sentiment swung towards the exiled Charles II. In May 1660 the king triumphantly returned amid popular rejoicing but pressing affairs of state did not prevent him from remembering his Cornish followers. Grenville was rewarded with the impressively sounding titles of Earl of Bath, Viscount Lansdowne and Baron of Bideford and Kilkhampton, while the borough of Penzance, which had staged a last defiant revolt in 1648, was elevated to the status of a Coinage Town. Others attempted to seek favour, like the men of Fowey who petitioned the king and reminded him of their devotion to the loyalist cause, wisely refraining from reference to one of their own, Hugh Peters, who had signed the famous death warrant which had sent his father to meet the executioner's axe. Peters, in fact, met a similar fate, as did two other leading Cornish republicans, John Carew and Gregory Clement, who were tried and executed in October 1660. At the administrative level, meanwhile, the institution of the Duchy, which had been abolished during Cromwell's Protectorate, was re-established and the Crown reasserted its traditional control over the increasingly lucrative tin trade.

*Quaker's Meeting House near Feock*

With the king and Duchy restored Cornwall returned to normality, although decades of constitutional and political debate had made little impact on a population which had shown little sympathy or even understanding of the wider issues at stake. Religious life, however, had been greatly stimulated by the ferment of new ideas and Puritanism, the desire for simplicity of worship, had been gaining ground among the Cornish since the 1640s. The impact on the clergy, too, had been small, and during the Interregnum scores of priests had to be ejected from their livings for refusing to submit to the rule of Parliament and the newly-imposed Covenant. While many were later reinstated, the lack of sufficient Parliamentarian clergy to fill the vacant posts in the short term had undermined the authority of the established church and helped to create a climate in which the dissenting sects began to make an impression on the ordinary people. The Quakers were the first to emerge in Cornwall, many suffering physical beatings for their beliefs, while the Presbyterians, Independents and Baptists also built up a following. Religious passion also came to be aroused over the plight of Bishop Jonathan Trelawny, sent to the Tower by James II for protesting against the 1687 Declaration of Indulgence which granted toleration to Catholics. His plight gave birth to a threatened march to London, immortalised in the *Song of the Western Men* and the words 'And shall Trelawny die? Here's 20,000 Cornishmen will know the reason why'. In the light of the experiences of 1497 and 1549 it is probably fortunate that the expedition never materialised; James' successor, William of Orange, had the bishop released and elevated to the See of Exeter. Protestantism in England was now triumphant, although in Cornwall the religious debate was to take on a new form half a century later with the appearance of Wesleyan Methodism.

*R. S. Hawker's depiction of Bishop Trelawny*

71

# IX  The Cornish Language: An Tavas Kernewek

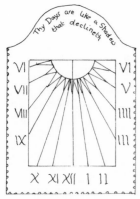

*A sundial from
Madron church*

The visitor to modern Cornwall is immediately confronted with evidence that this most westerly county of Britain has a linguistic heritage all of its own. The county border is dotted with bilingual signs which read *Kernow* as well as 'Cornwall', while place-names like Marazanvose, Ardensawah, Halabezack and Perranarworthal, sounding mysterious and sometimes unpronounceable to the outsider, stand in marked contrast to those of neighbouring Devon. Of all the counties of England, in fact, Cornwall has the unique distinction of possessing its own language which, although it died out as a spoken tongue in the late 18th century, is still vigorously nurtured as the single most important manifestation of Cornish identity.

Cornish is descended from the primitive Celtic which was spoken throughout most of Britain before the Anglo-Saxons began their colonisation of the south-east in the fourth and fifth centuries. As the newcomers spread out, the Celtic dialects gradually retreated into the peripheral regions and slowly came to assume the status of separate languages. By the end of the Dark Ages the northern and western branches of Celtic had developed into Gaelic, Irish and Manx, while the southern or Brythonic dialects had emerged as Welsh and Cornish, and a sixth variation, as we saw in Chapter Two, had in the meantime been carried overseas to Brittany. On mainland Britain pockets of isolated Celtic speakers survived elsewhere for a time, particularly in Cumberland and perhaps in the South Hams of Devon, but by the 11th and 12th centuries these had all but disappeared, leaving the surviving strains of Celtic confined to the remoteness of Scotland, Wales and Cornwall.

At the very time Cornish was developing into a separate language it was already in a state of retreat. The early Saxon incursions across the Tamar had drive the language out of the north-east where 90 per cent of the place-names are Old English, while it had also lost ground in the area between the Tamar and the Lynher where only 50 per cent of place-names are Cornish. By the time of the Norman Conquest pockets of English speakers could be found well within Celtic territory, but these were still a minority and, west of the Lynher, Cornish was commonly spoken throughout the early Middle Ages, not only by the peasants but also by the gentry; in the early 13th century a certain Richard 'of noble blood' was recommended for a high position to Bishop Grosseteste of Exeter but we are told that he could speak no English. By the end of the century, however, Cornish was beginning to

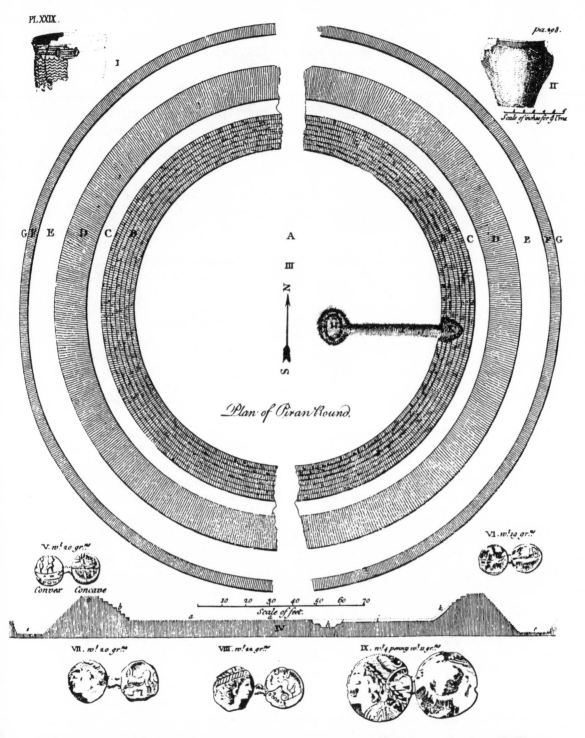

Piran (Perran) Round: the best preserved *plen-an-gwary* in Cornwall. This reproduction of William Borlase's drawing shows the seven rows of seats from which 2,000 people could watch the Miracle Plays being performed.

lose further ground in the east. Place-name forms are instructive in tracing this decline, as we find older forms of the language preserved, for example, in the word *cuit* meaning a 'wood'; in east Cornwall this appears in names like Penquite and Trequite, but across the central parts of the county we find the Middle Cornish *cos* in evidence in names like Tregoose and Pencoose. There are over a dozen places called Penquite east of Par and 10 to the west of it called Pencoose and, since this change from 't' to 's' was beginning *c*. 1100, it indicates that the language was already disappearing from much of the east by this time.

A second pointer to this decline in the east is the distribution of the *plen-an-gwary* or 'playing-places' in which the Cornish-language Miracle Plays were performed. There are very few *plen* east of Truro but several in the west, which suggests that the plays, which date from the mid-14th century, were rarely if ever performed in the eastern parishes. This is not to argue that Cornish had disappeared completely from mid Cornwall by 1400, but that English had become more common and there were insufficient Cornish-speakers to warrant the players' attention. The records of the Bishops of Exeter, in fact, show that the language still retained some ground in mid Cornwall during the 14th century; reference is made to Ralph de Tremur of Lanivet, near Bodmin, who was a fluent Cornish-speaker, while in 1339 a licence to preach was granted to John Polmark to help the vicar of St Merryn near Padstow 'expound the word of God in the said church in the Cornish language'. Again, among the penitentiaries appointed for the archdeaconry of Cornwall in 1355 was a certain Brother John at Bodmin who was to hear confessions for those who knew both languages, while Brother Roger de Tyrel of Truro was to administer to those who knew nothing but Cornish. Further west, most of the population still knew very little, if any, English, and when Bishop Grandisson visited St Buryan in 1336 he found it necessary to appoint the vicar of St Just as his interpreter since many of the inhabitants spoke only Cornish.

Observations on the state of the language become more frequent from the early 16th century. In 1538 Sir William Godolphin responded to a request from Thomas Cromwell to send him some expert tinners, but had to point out that it would be necessary to 'call [John] Herry to interpret these men's languages for their English is very bad'. Andrew Boorde, in 1542, confirmed that there were still many monoglot Cornish speakers. In his *Fyrst Boke of the Introduction of knowledge* he observed that 'In Cornwall is two speches: the one is naughty [i.e. corrupt] Englysshe, and the other is Cornysshe speche. And there may be many men and women the whiche cannot speake one worde of Englysshe, but all Cornysshe'. Unfortunately Boorde gave no indication of the geographical extent of spoken Cornish, adding only a few sentences in the language, the numerals up to 30, and a few damaging comments on Cornish food and, above all, the beer which was

*A Cornish milestone*

'thick and smoky and also it is thin,
It is like wash as pigs had wrestled therein'!

We do not know where Boorde stayed and his comments may even
have been second-hand, as there can be no doubt that English was
supplanting the old tongue. The increasing bilingualism even west of
Truro is revealed by an ecclesiastical court case at Lelant in 1572 when
'the wife of Morrysh David called Agnes Davey "whore and whore
bitch" in English and not in Cornowok'. The religious upheavals of
the 16th century, with no Cornish version of the Bible or the Book of
Common Prayer, clearly had great effect, and in his *Survey* of 1602
Richard Carew outlined the territorial retreat which had taken place,
noting that 'the English speech doth still encroach upon it and hath
driven the same into the uttermost skirts of the shire'.

*A decorated bench-end
from St Winnow's
church*

The loss of the language in the 17th century was probably greater
than at any time before. The Miracle Plays ceased to be performed and
we are told by John Norden early in the century that even in the far
west most people were now bilingual, while Cornish had virtually
disappeared east of Truro: 'In the west parte of the county, as in the
Hundreds of Penwith and Kerrier, the Cornish tongue is mostly in use,
and it is to be marvelled that though husband and wife, parents and
children, master and servantes doe mutually communicate in their
native language, yet there is none of them but in manner is able to
converse with a stranger in the English tongue, unless it be some obscure
persons that seldom converse with the better sort. But it seemeth that in
a few years the Cornish language will be by little and little abandoned'.
Norden's observations, though, clearly show that the linguistic division
was also becoming a class one and that Cornish was being seen as an
obstacle to social advancement. The 'obscure persons' could not keep
it alive for long and we are not surprised to read in John Ray's *Itinerary*
of 1662 that few of 'the children could speak Cornish, so that the
language is like, in a short time, to be quite lost'.

The local antiquary William Scawen, writing in the 1670s, was very
informative about the position of Cornish in his day, saying that it was
still used in the western promontories of Penwith and the Lizard, but
adding that it was in terminal decline: 'It may, I confess, be lamented,
and heavily laid to the charge of us and our ancestors . . . to have been
much wanting to ourselves in the loss of the Cornish speech'. Another
commentator, Nicholas Boson of Newlyn near Penzance, reinforces
the increasing social castigation of the language which Norden hinted
at. Boson wrote a short pamphlet entitled *Nebbaz Gerriau dro tho
Carnoack* ('A few words about Cornish') in which he says that he was
prevented from acquiring a knowledge of it before he was six years old
by his mother, who had insisted that the servants should not speak it
to him. In this work of *c.* 1700 he reveals that the Cornish-speaking
district now only extended along the shores of Mount's Bay, the Lizard,
and around St Ives, but that the area had considerably receded in his

lifetime. The Welsh antiquary Edward Lhuyd, who spent some months in Cornwall at about the time Boson was writing, recorded the names of 24 parishes in which the language was still spoken, but added that 'a great many of the inhabitants of those parishes, especially the gentry, do not understand it, and everyone is able to speak good English'.

The final demise of Cornish in the 18th century was rapid. By 1735 two local scholars, Gwavas and Tonkin, could find only a few speakers in the small fishing villages and coves between Penzance and Land's End, and it was in one of these, Mousehole, that the old Celtic tongue finally died. This was the home of an aged *jowster* or fish hawker called Dolly Pentreath, who is the last known native speaker of Cornish. Dolly died in 1777, but nine years before her death she was visited by the antiquary Daines Barrington who noticed that there were still other folk in the village who understood her, but could not speak the language readily. Dolly's place in the history books was confirmed in 1860 when a bilingual tombstone in Paul churchyard was erected to her memory by Prince Louis Lucien Bonaparte, a descendant of Napoleon and a keen antiquary.

*Dolly Pentreath, last native speaker of Cornish*

Although Dolly was probably the last person to speak Cornish fluently, knowledge of the language lingered on for a little longer. Her epitaph had been written by a Truro mining engineer called Thomson who was evidently well versed in it, while another Mousehole inhabitant, a fisherman called William Bodener, could speak Cornish after a fashion. In 1776, 13 years before his death, he had written to Barrington saying 'My age is three-score and five. I am a poor fisherman. I learnt Cornish when I was a boy. I have been to sea with my father and five other men in the boat, and we have not heard one word of English spoke in the boat, for a week together. I never saw a Cornish book. I learned Cornish going to sea with old men, there is not more than four or five in our town can talk Cornish now old people four-score years old. Cornish is all forgot with young people'.

Bodener, like many others, left children who were able to count in Cornish and recite a few phrases, but he appears to have been one of the last with any conversational knowledge of the language, although spotting the alleged 'final speaker' became a popular pastime among antiquarians at the end of the 18th century. John Tremethack, who died in 1852, knew enough to teach a few phrases to his daughter who was still alive in 1875, while John Davey of Boswednack near Zennor, who died in 1891, was also reputed to have been able to recite traditional rhymes and verses. While there are many other examples, some rather suspect, the final word must rest with the celebrated Cornish scholar, R. Morton Nance: 'We must accept 1800 as being about the very latest date at which anyone really spoke Cornish traditionally, as even the remnant of a living language, all traditional Cornish since then having been learned parrot-wise from those of an earlier generation'.

Now that we have reviewed the history of the language, it might be worthwhile to consider the question, 'why did Cornish die out?'.

76

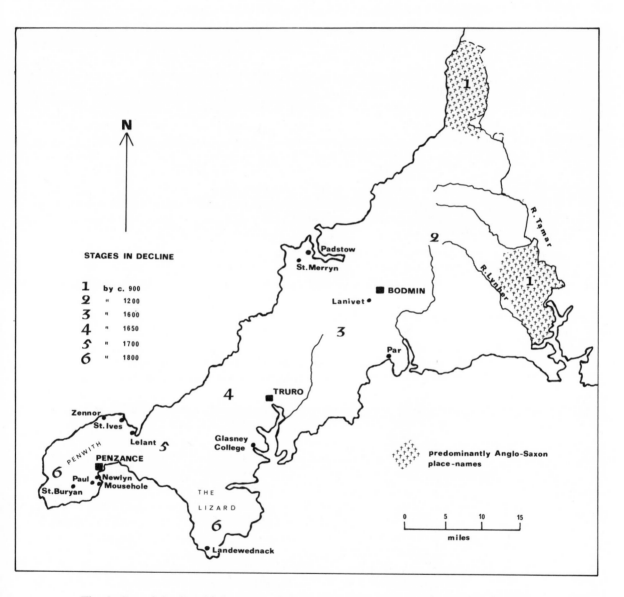

The decline of the Cornish language, showing towns and villages mentioned in the text.

77

Inevitably its decline was the result of a complex weave of social, political and religious factors, and at an early stage the displacement of the Cornish land-holding classes by the Saxons and then the Normans was crucial. The relegation of the native Cornish to inferior positions in society is shown by the 10th- and 11th-century glosses in the 'Bodmin Gospels', which record the manumission or freeing of slaves; while 98 of the slaves' names are Cornish, those of the manumittors are mostly Anglo-Saxon. Admittedly, some of the Cornish upper classes adopted the personal names of their political masters, but the point remains that the Cornish were a subjected people. Domesday Book, too, shows that by 1066 only six men with Cornish names remained as landholders, while 20 years later there were even fewer. Those outsiders, who replaced them and established family lines which often survived for centuries, failed to provide similar patronage to that which allowed Welsh to flourish as a language of poetry and learning. As a result of this social rift, Cornish became synonymous with the language of the peasants, the speech of the ignorant and illiterate. As William Scawen of Saltash put it in 1680, 'the poor speak Cornish, but are laughed at by the rich that speak it not'. The great religious changes of the 16th century also speeded up the process of anglicisation; whereas the first Welsh books were printed in the 1540s with a translation of both the Bible and the Prayer Book, no one seriously listened to the Cornish rebels in 1549 when they asked for a version in their native tongue. The Cornish men of learning, moreover, had little time for the language and did even less to foster it. Richard Carew, described by A. L. Rowse as 'our chief literary light in that Age', was a great Renaissance scholar well versed in Greek, Latin, Italian, French and Spanish, but in his *Survey* of 1602 he allocated only a few pages to a language which was clearly only a curiosity to him, and it is significant that another of his famous works was none other than 'An Epistle concerning the Excellencies of the English Tongue'. Other events also played their part in the final demise of the language, like the use of the Cornish ports, which already contained a large proportion of foreigners, to fight the Spaniards. The persecution of Catholics, too, put an end to the thousand-year intercourse with Celtic-speaking Brittany which had done much to sustain Cornish. In 1498 Bretons had constituted 63 per cent of all maritime traffic at Padstow and a staggering 94 per cent in Mount's Bay, while the Breton scholar Joseph Loth estimated the Breton element in the population of Penwith just before the Reformation to have been as high as one-sixth.

All these changes, together with the impact of the Civil War which Charles Thomas has shown to have accounted for the death of the language on the Scillies, disturbed the tranquility of Cornwall which had sheltered Cornish for so long. The westward expansion of the tin and copper industries likewise played a part in the final stages; as the workings of east Cornwall became exhausted new mines opened up in the west and large numbers of English-speaking tinners moved into

*Antony House, ancestral home of the Carews*

Penwith and Kerrier where the language still stubbornly survived. As a result, Cornish speakers in the inland parishes became swamped and the language was finally left to die on the lips of the fisher folk. Even at its height, Cornish was restricted to a small geographical area and could hardly have boasted more than, perhaps, 30,000 speakers.

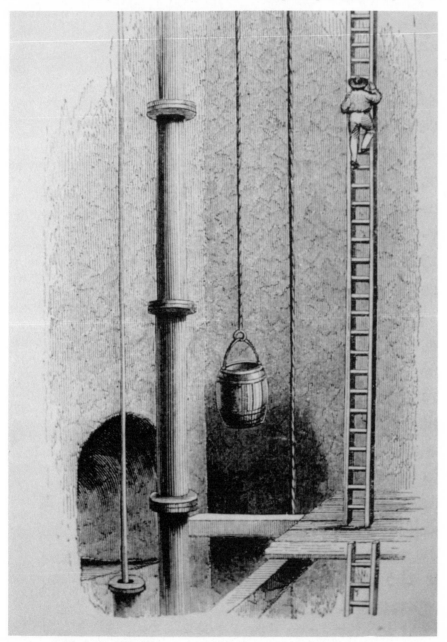

Fig. 3. A rather spacious impression of a tin mine, showing the engine pump and the 'kibbles' used to bring the ore to the surface. The entrance on the left was probably to a level.

# X A Living from the Sea

*Captain Bligh of the Bounty: a seafarer with Cornish connections*

The sea has always been a major influence on Cornwall's development. Throughout prehistory and well beyond medieval times it afforded a superior avenue for immigration, communication and commerce when overland travel was tedious, cumbersome and at times well nigh impossible. It has provided generations of merchants, mariners and fishermen with a living, if often a tenuous one, and continues to determine the very identity and personality of the county in the eyes of the outside world.

The title of this chapter quite literally covers a multitude of sins, for the coastal communities of Cornwall have not always exploited the sea with due regard to the finer points of English law. Piracy, smuggling and wrecking may well have entered the annals of Cornish folklore and provided the substance of countless popular books, but in the days of remoteness from officialdom they all played a very real part in the growth of a flourishing clandestine economy. Piracy was endemic along the whole Channel coast from the 14th to the 17th centuries. As early as 1348 the practice was sufficiently established for the archdeacon of Cornwall to receive a royal mandate instructing him 'to take action against the pirates who infested the Cornish waters', while the monks of Tresco abbey were forced to complain of being exposed to the 'many privateers and their vices' who frequented the Scillies. The peak of piracy, however, came later, during the 16th and 17th centuries when a complex organisation grew up between the Cornish pirates and those of Wales. The trade was controlled and the merchandise disposed of by the gentry, attracted by the prospect of £1,000 cargoes, while the pirates generally received only about one-fifth of the haul.

The most important target for the pirates appears to have been coastal traffic; Spanish and Gascon wines, wheat and salt, were in great demand and easily disposed of. The Fal and Helford estuaries, with their numerous coves and creeks, were ideally suited to the trade, and prominent local families like the Killigrews of Arwenack were heavily involved. In 1557 three members of the family attacked a vessel off Land's End and seized its £10,000 cargo, while in 1582 Lady Killigrew and her household boarded another, removed the cargo and drowned most of the crew. The Killigrews also had relatives in high places in South Wales, including John Godolphin, steward of Laugharne, and Sir John Wogan, none other than the vice-admiral of South Wales, and between them they established a complex operation which took in scores of easily corruptible government officials and lesser landowners. Piracy, however, was far from a one-sided profession, and the activities of the infamous Turks caused considerable distress on many occasions; in 1625 Looe lost 80 inhabitants to these slavers and there are many references to the entire crews of fishing boats being seized and never heard of again. By the mid-17th century, however, organised piracy was fast declining. The wars against Spain had not only reduced the number of Spanish ships venturing into English waters but caused large concentrations of British warships to be stationed off the south-west ports which made the work of the pirates much more difficult. By 1700 the privateers had all but disappeared from Cornwall, and fortunately so had the Turks.

If plundering a vessel on the high seas failed to offend the Cornish conscience, pillaging others driven onto the rocks did not either, and it is quite clear that wrecking was a common enough practice along all parts of the county's hazardous coastline. Much has been written about the subject, perhaps as much fiction as historical fact, but we are still dealing with a practice which, legends aside, can be accurately documented from an early date. For many coastal communities this was not just an occasional pursuit but often an essential ingredient of their otherwise meagre and precarious lives. All sections of society put great value on what turned up on Cornwall's shores, and the Revd. John Troutbeck aptly summed up the popular feeling of many communities with the plea, 'We pray Thee, O Lord, not that wrecks should happen, but that if wrecks do happen, Thou wilt guide them into the Scilly Isles, for the benefit of the poor inhabitants'! Traditionally a shipwrecked vessel and its contents belonged to the Crown or to the lord of the manor, although local custom dictated that half of the spoils belonged to the salvors.

This is clear from the plight of the *Gabriell* of Milford Haven, driven onto Wolf Rock in 1394. Her merchandise, valued at £1,000, was washed ashore and we are told that 'the men of those parts removed the cargo as wreck . . . and refuse to restore it'. Gradually the right of wreck passed into the hands of the lords of coastal manors such as Connerton which came to control this valuable privilege over the treacherous shoreline around Land's End. In the case of the equally dangerous Lizard peninsula the right was parcelled between the manors of Methleigh, Winnianton and Predannack, and the records contain several references to these catastrophes. During the 15th and 16th centuries, in particular, many Spanish, Flemish and Portuguese treasure ships were washed ashore, including the *St Anthony*, en route from Flanders to Plymouth, which was wrecked at Gunwalloe in January 1526 carrying £16,000 worth of bullion and silver.

*The Longships lighthouse*

In a genuine effort to prevent such mishaps, several primitive lighthouses were erected on some of the most notorious headlands, usually by priests or benevolent town gilds. Charles Henderson suggested that

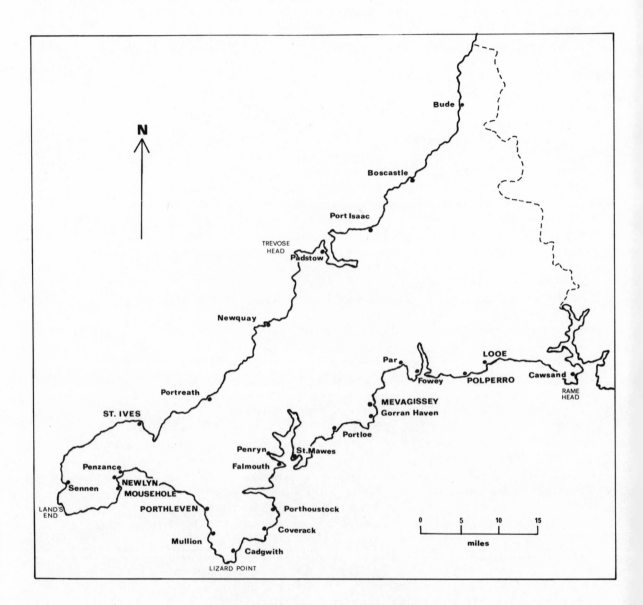

Fishing communities in the 19th century.

82

the coastal chapels which overlooked Hayle, Bude, St Ives and Rame Head may have been erected for this purpose, and this function may also have been associated with the medieval chapel which stood on the summit of Chapel Carn Brea, towering over Land's End and Cape Cornwall. There is documentary evidence, again, of a light on St Michael's Mount from the 1430s. Such Christian considerations, on the other hand, were rarely shared by the local people, and when a lighthouse was built at the Lizard in 1619 they complained that it took away 'God's grace from them; meaning that they now shall receive no more benefit from shipwreck. They have been so long used to reap profit by the calamity of the ruin of shipping, that they claim it as hereditary'.

*An early lighthouse from St Michael's Mount*

Wrecking gradually died out during the early 19th century as a consequence of a more efficient coastguard service and an increase in the number of lighthouses along the more notorious lengths of coastline. Its end was contemporary with the decline of another pursuit, smuggling. Although there are several medieval indications of this practice, smuggling on a large scale developed in the late 16th century and, according to one authority, G. N. Clark, the smugglers' share in national commerce soon amounted to as much as one third of the legitimate traffic. In Cornwall's case, most early smuggling was actually out of the county when the principal commodity was tin. Since 1198 all tin had been liable to a royal tax, and it is clear that large quantities were illegally exported to avoid paying the duty. Penzance appears to have been heavily involved in this activity, and Belgium and Italy were the chief markets. Economic historians have concluded that this illicit trade had assumed such formidable proportions by the end of the 16th century that it renders the official tin production figures inadequate barometers of the true state of the industry. By the middle of the following century, however, the government was making a determined effort to curb tin smuggling by appointing smelting supervisors to make sure that each smelting works could account for every block produced. Not surprisingly, we learn from the correspondence of one supervisor-general, George Treweek, that this was a daunting task, not least because of minimal co-operation from the interested parties.

Cornish smuggling was at its peak in the 18th century, when it had assumed the proportions of a major industry rather than an occasional sideline. High import duties which often doubled the price of some commodities, like tea, an expanding and more prosperous gentry class with a growing appetite for the fineries of life, and a hopelessly inadequate customs service all contributed to its success. Highly organised bands, more often than not in league with local officials, brought in large quantities of spirits, tobacco, silks, laces, and French salt, much preferred by the pilchard curers but heavily taxed by the government. As with the privateers, a complex network was established with Brittany and the Channel Islands, and the exploits of some individual smugglers assumed legendary proportions. High in the ranks of the

*A smuggler*

infamous was John Carter, locally known as the 'King of Prussia', who operated from the little Mount's Bay inlet at Porthleah, known ever since as 'Prussia Cove'.

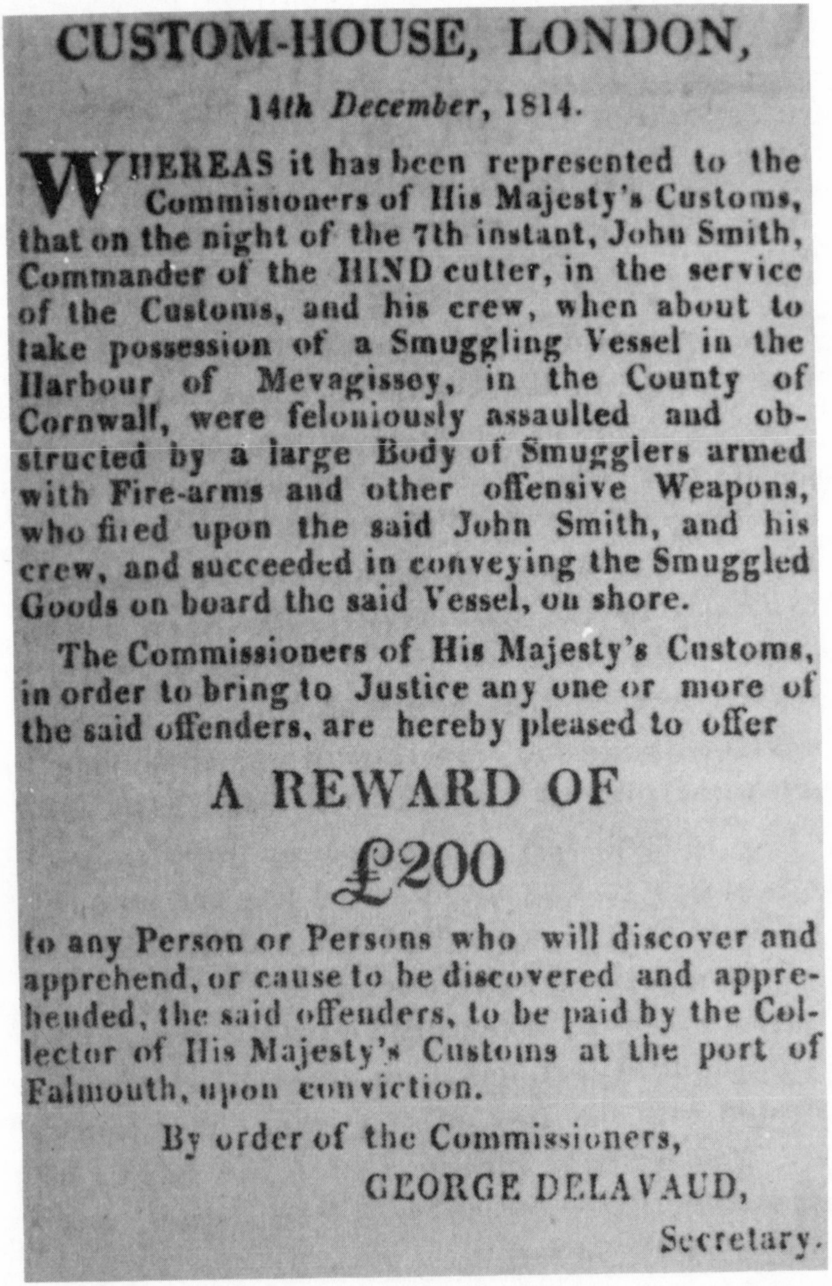

## CUSTOM-HOUSE, LONDON,

### 14th December, 1814.

WHEREAS it has been represented to the Commissioners of His Majesty's Customs, that on the night of the 7th instant, John Smith, Commander of the HIND cutter, in the service of the Customs, and his crew, when about to take possession of a Smuggling Vessel in the Harbour of Mevagissey, in the County of Cornwall, were feloniously assaulted and obstructed by a large Body of Smugglers armed with Fire-arms and other offensive Weapons, who fired upon the said John Smith, and his crew, and succeeded in conveying the Smuggled Goods on board the said Vessel, on shore.

The Commissioners of His Majesty's Customs, in order to bring to Justice any one or more of the said offenders, are hereby pleased to offer

## A REWARD OF

## £200

to any Person or Persons who will discover and apprehend, or cause to be discovered and apprehended, the said offenders, to be paid by the Collector of His Majesty's Customs at the port of Falmouth, upon conviction.

By order of the Commissioners,

GEORGE DELAVAUD,

Secretary.

Fig. 4. Government rewards like this one of 1814 did little to deter smugglers.

In spite of the increased efforts of the Revenue cutters and the Preventive boats, it proved impossible for the authorities to curtail the scale of smuggling. Corruption at high levels, hostile and tightly-knit communities, an elaborate network of landing and storage places, all were insuperable barriers. Even the offer of very substantial rewards, untold riches by the standards of the day, like the £200 which followed an incident at Mevagissey in 1814 and £500 following an attack on a customs man in 1831, made very little impact. Even when offenders were actually arrested, the old saying that 'a Cornish jury will never convict a smuggler' points to the difficulty in securing a conviction. Some parts of the county were more involved in the trade than others and the south coast, closer to France and the Channel Islands and with more secluded landing places, was easily preferred. The shores of Mount's Bay provided many a haven, particularly around Mullion, while the men of the Scillies were the most notorious of all. A determined effort to stamp out smuggling from the islands was so successful that in 1818 the magistrates of Penwith reported that the islanders were in a state of abject poverty; 'for generations [they] had been brought up in this mode of support' but had now lost 'almost every comfort'. By this time, in fact, the days of large-scale smuggling everywhere were numbered and the end of the war against Napoleon allowed the government to concentrate its naval resources against the contraband trade, and a new Preventive force was established. Their renewed efforts, coupled with the triumph of free trade, proved decisive. During the 1840s Robert Peel reduced the import duties on hundreds of foreign items which helped to remove the economic base of most smuggling operations. Small-scale activities continued, as shown by the arrest of several St Ives fishermen for tobacco smuggling in 1884, but the advent of a more law-abiding age and the strict rigours of Methodism ensured that they would not return.

The more legitimate activity of fishing, from such a long and indented coastline, has made a substantial contribution to the local economy. For thousands of years and from scores of natural havens men have ventured out, in the words of the 16th-century antiquary John Norden, to take advantage of the 'greate store and manie kindes of verie excellent fishe, whose particular names are infinite'. The exploitation of the sea and shoreline from the Mesolithic period onwards has now been well established by archaeologists. Several prehistoric sites have yielded large numbers of limpets, cockles, mussels and crabs, as well as a wide variety of whitefish bones from the waste tips or middens.Primitive nets and long-lines, probably baited with limpets, appear to have been in use during the Iron Age, and were probably set both from the shore and from small skin-covered vessels. These practices are assumed to have continued throughout the Romano–British and early medieval periods, though very little evidence has come to light. There is no documentary evidence, and very few later coastal sites have been excavated except for Mawgan Porth which shed little light on the

*A traditional Cornish 'ink-well' lobster pot*

*A pilchard drifter*

subject. We learn nothing about sea-fishing, either, from Domesday Book although its compilers were concerned with sources of manorial income, so the omission is not significant. At the same time we should not ignore the references to freshwater fisheries; medieval lords attached great importance to their weirs which trapped salmon, eels and trout along the Tamar, Lynher and other main rivers. Oysters from the Fal estuary were also in demand from at least the late 13th century, when they were being shipped to Exeter, Bristol and other up-country markets.

By this time the picture for the wider sea-fishing industry is beginning to clear. In 1202 King John granted licences to three merchants from Bayonne to fish 'for whales, conger and hake, from St Michael's Mount to Dartmouth', and by 1213 Bayonnese and Gascon merchants had come to control much of the Cornish market. Henry III's Cornish poet, Michael Blakenpayne, was able to write of his native county in the mid-13th century, 'In fish and tin she knows no rival coast', a conclusion which others had also reached, and we know from a charter granted to Guernsey fishermen in 1288 that they regularly fished the Cornish waters for mackerel and conger. The native contribution to the industry was also expanding, and from a Survey of the Manor of Alverton of 1327 we learn that there were 13 fishing boats at Penzance and 16 at Mousehole. Ten years later the men of St Ives were paying a Port Farm, an annual render to the Duchy calculated according to the number of fishing boats of £6, while the Mount's Bay boats paid just over £9 between them. Fishing had clearly progressed from an occasional pursuit into a well organised commercial concern, and after tin it was Cornwall's most important medieval export; in 1438 over £1,000-worth was sent abroad, not to mention that which must have gone to other parts of England. Hake was the single most sought-after species at this time, although by the early 16th century the fish had changed its migratory habits and had been replaced by pilchards.

The humble pilchard was to have a profound effect on Cornwall's coastal communities. By 1602 it had become so plentiful that Richard Carew was able to assert that 'the least fish in bignes, greatest for gain, and most in number, is the Pilchard'. Exports had already risen to *c.* 600 tons p.a. and the industry and its organisation had assumed all the trappings of a capitalist enterprise. The season usually began in late July and extended until the end of the year, occasionally into January and February. The traditional catching method involved the use of a huge seine net weighing up to three tons, and the operation was directed either by a small boat known as a 'lurker' or from the shore by the 'huers'. The seine boat and its attendant craft would be allocated a particular length of the coast or 'stem' at the beginning of each season and would wait at anchor until the huers on the cliff-top identified an approaching shoal from the distinctive colour the fish made in the water. The sighting would be followed by the cry of 'hevva' which would arouse the whole village as well as the waiting seiners. The whole

*The Huer's House, Newquay*

86

operation of encircling the shoal and casting the net was then directed by the huers using two 'bushes' which were employed in a kind of semaphore manner. The ends of the seine were then drawn tight by 'blowsers' working from the shore and the whole net, with the pilchards trapped inside, was then anchored to the sea bed. Once secured, the fish had to be removed from the seine by a process known as 'tucking', which involved bringing proportions of the trapped fish to the surface in a small net and then scooping the catch from the water in wicker baskets. The pilchards were then carried ashore for curing, and if the shoal was a large one, the whole process could last for several days.

*A huer directing the fleet with 'bushes'*

As the local market was only capable of absorbing a small proportion of the catch, from the earliest days of the industry methods of preserving the fish had to be employed. Smoking or 'fuming' was common in Tudor times and the process gave rise to the term 'fumadoes', corrupted into 'fairmaids', as the local name for pilchards. Pickling in brine was also common at this time, but by the late 18th century dry-salting or 'bulking' had become the norm throughout the county. This involved transporting the fish to specially-built cellars or 'palaces'; in his *Tour* of 1780 the Revd. John Swete described the next stage: 'their method of curing them is to place them whole in large bulks for many days; they are then washed and placed under large stone weights, by the gentle pressure of which large quantities of the common train oil are drained from them into proper vessels. They are then pickled and prest into barrels'. This pressing into barrels or 'hogsheads' took about a week, after which they were sealed and made ready for market. The whole process was clearly very labour intensive, and during the second half of the 19th century a more efficient method of curing in large tanks was adopted from Spain, although it was unpopular among the fisherfolk, and there were complaints of a deterioration in the quality of the final product.

The greater part of the pilchard catch was exported, initially to the West Indies and then to the Mediterranean world, especially Italy. With the eating of meat during Lent forbidden by the Catholic Church, pilchards were a cheap and ready alternative, prompting many an offering of the old toast:

> 'Here's a health to the Pope, and may he repent,
> And lengthen by six months the term of his Lent.
> It's always declared, betwixt the two poles,
> There's nothing like pilchards for saving of souls'.

Fishing has always been a precarious livelihood, and though today's fishermen are capable of adapting their gear and methods according to market demands and the seasonal movements of different species, their 18th- and 19th-century counterparts were less flexible. Pilchard seining involved vast capital investment on the part of the many business consortiums who owned the seines and, beyond the odd shoal of mackerel, the equipment was unsuitable for any other work. As a

*A Mount's Bay lugger*

result, when there were no pilchards there was no work, and there are huge variations in the annual catch figures. The second half of the 18th century saw a prolonged national decline in the industry, and fish exports fell from 2.6 per cent of total exports in 1722 to only 0.7 per cent by 1772. While the respective statistics for Cornwall are far from complete, the picture seems to have been little different. In 1786, only 7,000 hogsheads left Cornish ports, although by the end of the century there had been a dramatic recovery with 65,000 hogsheads exported in 1796. No one port illustrates these fluctuating fortunes better than St Ives, the county's premier pilchard station throughout the following century. A Board of Trade enquiry of 1874 listed a total of 272 boats operating from the port which employed 1551 men, not to mention the hundreds of women and children who were traditionally involved in the curing processes. Sometimes no shoals were spotted for years on end, as was the case between 1818–22, while at other times the catches could assume staggering proportions. In October 1851 the 'Hope' seine netted a huge shoal which took a fortnight to remove from the water and to process, and at the end of the whole operation some 5,600 hogsheads had been packed, representing 18 million pilchards. The price was 45s. 0d. per hogshead, quite a fair one, which meant a grand total of £12,600, and a profit after expenses of £7,569. Another substantial catch, this time of 8,000 hogsheads, was landed at Newquay in October 1866, but these were exceptions, and it was more usual to count catches in hundreds of hogsheads, not thousands.

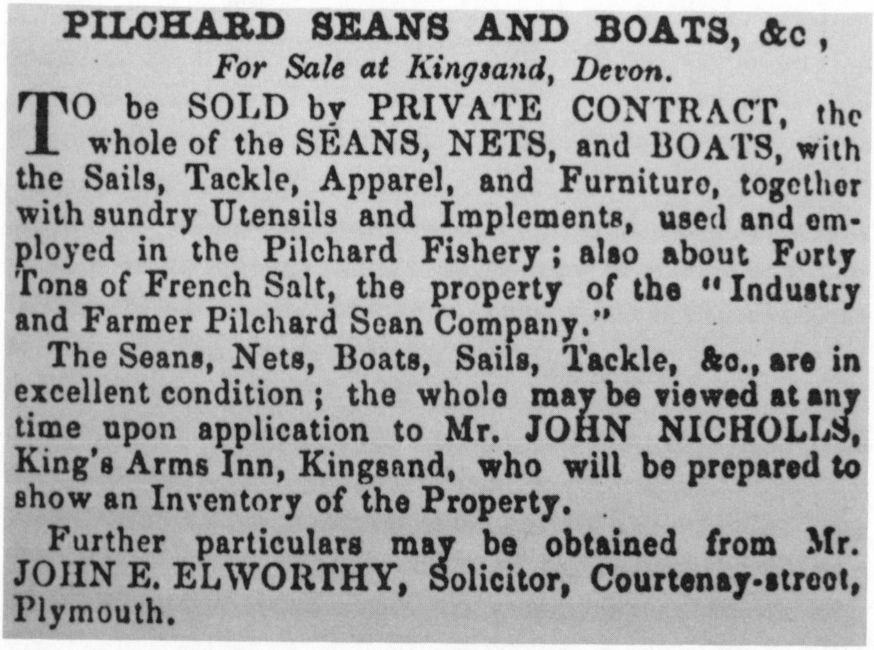

**PILCHARD SEANS AND BOATS, &c,**

*For Sale at Kingsand, Devon.*

TO be SOLD by PRIVATE CONTRACT, the whole of the SEANS, NETS, and BOATS, with the Sails, Tackle, Apparel, and Furniture, together with sundry Utensils and Implements, used and employed in the Pilchard Fishery; also about Forty Tons of French Salt, the property of the "Industry and Farmer Pilchard Sean Company."

The Seans, Nets, Boats, Sails, Tackle, &c., are in excellent condition; the whole may be viewed at any time upon application to Mr. JOHN NICHOLLS, King's Arms Inn, Kingsand, who will be prepared to show an Inventory of the Property.

Further particulars may be obtained from Mr. JOHN E. ELWORTHY, Solicitor, Courtenay-street, Plymouth.

Fig. 5. The West Country press was full of advertisements like this once pilchard seining began to collapse in the 1870s.

During the late 1870s pilchard seining fell into rapid decline, having already disappeared from most of the south coast. In 1878 only 170 hogsheads were processed in the entire county, and the newspapers were full of advertisements as the owners tried to dispose of their boats and nets before the situation deteriorated still further. What

Fig. 6. An early 19th-century fishwife bearing the once-familiar 'cowel'.

caused this decline is uncertain; some blamed a slight change in the direction of the Gulf Stream which took the fish and their feed elsewhere, others blamed the recent increase in drift net fishing which had been causing friction for some time. Drift netting involved working in deeper waters and setting long lengths, sometimes as much as a mile, of finely-meshed net just below the surface, usually just before sunset when the pilchards rose to feed. The seiners argued that this method dispersed the shoals before they could move inshore and from the earliest days of drifting there had been attempts to curtail it. In 1841 the St Ives seine owners secured the passing of a local Fishery Act which outlawed drift netting between 25 July and 25 December within 2,400 yards of the coast, but this and similar restraints had not prevented the number of drifters from increasing. Their methods also allowed greater flexibility and enabled the boats to take part in the Mount's Bay mackerel fishery, which expanded rapidly in the 1880s, attracting vessels not only from other Cornish ports but from Lowestoft and Yarmouth. The drifters could also fish the Irish waters for herring when things were slack at home and, set against this versatility and mobility, the old seining methods appealed less and less. The introduction, just before the First World War, of the internal combustion engine enabled the drifters to fish more distant waters and in worse weather, and within a few years seining had become a thing of the past. The St Ives men shot their last seine in 1928 and most of the fleet ignominiously ended as firewood. For the drifters, however, as we will see in the final chapter, their supremacy proved to be relatively short, and by the late 1950's 'King Pilchard' had all but deserted them as well.

*The old winch house at Sennen Cove*

# XI  Cornwall and her Industries

Above the door of the old *Tinner's Arms* in the little West Cornwall village of St Hilary formerly hung a wooden plaque which sported the verse . . .

> 'Come all good Cornish boys, walk in,
> Here's brandy, rum, and shrub, and gin,
> You can't do less than drink success
> To Copper, Fish and Tin'.

*An early lifeboat*

While the farmers, quarrymen and China clay workers may have been forgiven for taking an exception to their omission, this common toast aptly pinpointed the staple ingredients of the Cornish economy in the 18th and 19th centuries. The evidence, indeed, remains all around us, and while the old pilchard 'palaces' may have been converted beyond recognition to other uses, the landscape of much of the county is still dotted with scores of lofty, tapering chimneys, many with their attached engine houses, all poignant reminders of Cornwall's industrial past.

Tin is not by any means a common European mineral, and beyond the south west it is only found in Spain, Brittany and western Czechoslovakia. The ore, known as casserite, is associated with the kind of granite extrusions which run from Dartmoor to the Scillies, but it can also be found in the form of alluvial deposits in streams, the result of the weathering of the tin veins during the Ice Age. It was these secondary deposits, sifted from the stream beds, which provided the basis for the earliest phases of exploitation and in previous chapters we have already seen evidence of prehistoric activity and of the flourishing trade with the Mediterranean world in late Roman times. As to the fortunes of tinning throughout the Romano–British and early medieval periods, the picture is far from clear although it would be wise to envisage a fairly low-key pursuit, carried out by occasional tinners for the small domestic market.

Authentic documentation dates from 1156 when the Crown was already levying an annual tax on production. In 1198 a royal warden was appointed and three years later King John granted a charter which exempted the tinners from customary villein obligations and confirmed their rights of 'bounding', by which anyone could search for tin anywhere, so long as the landowner received a bounty, usually between one-tenth and one-fifteenth of the spoils. The centre of the industry by this time was also clearly shifting westwards — Cornwall had been

91

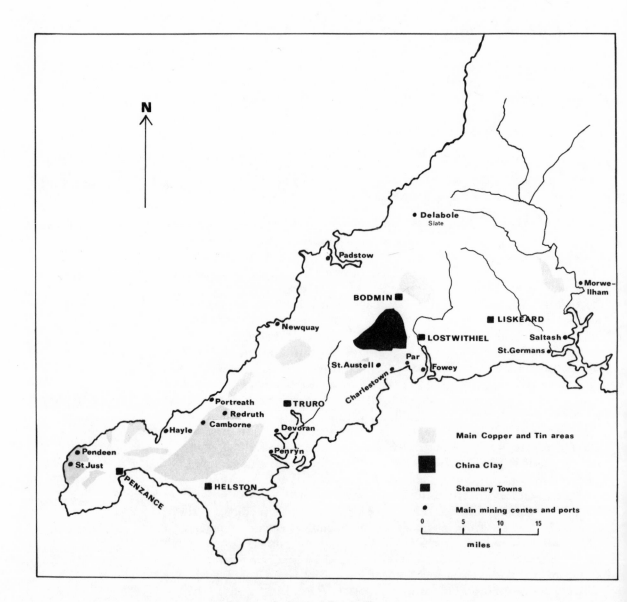

N

Main Copper and Tin areas

China Clay

Stannary Towns

Main mining centes and ports

0    5    10    15

miles

Industrial Cornwall.

92

overshadowed by west Devon in the early days — and by 1337 the annual output reached 700 tons. During the second half of the 14th century, however, production fell sharply as the Black Death took its human toll and disrupted economic life, and there was no substantial rise in the industry's fortunes until the 1460s, by which time the nature of tin extraction was changing. Most alluvial deposits had become exhausted, and medieval tinners had been increasingly forced to dig into the hillsides in search of new lodes. Shaft mining had also begun, but on a modest scale as miners were handicapped by their inability to solve the formidable drainage problems. By the early 1600s, however, elementary water pumps had been devised, mainly of the ingenious 'rag-and-chain' type, and the true tin 'mine' had become a reality. Smelting techniques, meanwhile, had also advanced and the old method of smelting the ore in a fire fuelled by turves had been superseded by the practice of 'blowing', by which the tin was smelted in stone furnaces and collected in moulds to form ingots of *c.* 200–300 lbs.

*The de Dunstanville monument, Carn Brea*

With the development of the industry came the creation of an elaborate legal and administrative framework which allowed the tinners to enjoy a substantial degree of autonomy. A succession of royal charters had bestowed important privileges, the right to hold their own courts, exemption from ordinary taxation, and even the authority to call their own 'Tinners' Parliament'. The county had also been divided into four stannary districts, and the Crown had designated certain stannary or coinage towns to which all tin had to be taken before it could be sold. Initially Lostwithiel, Liskeard, Truro, Helston and Bodmin acted as coinage centres, but the last named was abandoned as the industry moved westwards and in 1663 Penzance was added to the list in recognition of Penwith's increasing importance. Twice, later four times, a year the tin ingots would be taken to these centres, weighed and then 'coigned', by which a corner would be removed and analysed for impurities. During the early 15th century Cornwall's 3,000 tinners presented an average of 1¼ million lbs. for coinage each year which then sold at about £10–12 per 1,000 lbs. As the tax represented as much as 20 per cent of the total value, however, a substantial black-market trade had also grown up and large quantities were illicitly exported.

After a lengthy period of modest progress, the early 16th century saw the introduction of technical innovations which raised the curtain on a period of more substantial growth. Between 1460 and 1620, despite many sharp fluctuations, tin production doubled and, by the end of the 17th century, exports, at least the official ones, amounted to almost £100,000 a year. The Crown, particularly Elizabeth I, was keen to develop copper and lead resources, in Cumberland as well as Cornwall, and the Mines Royal Society had sponsored a number of exploratory ventures at Treworthy, Zennor and St Just. The ore was then shipped from St Ives to Neath in South Wales for smelting, but the enterprise was not a success and by the late 1580s the mines had

# DREADFUL ACCIDENT

## IN THE PARISH OF

# WENDRON

## TUESDAY AUGUST 24th 1858

## SEVEN LIVES LOST

**A sollard shaft collapsed filling the levels with thousands of cubic fathoms of *evil slime***

A great wind warns tributers and tut men, 43 escape up ladderways to grass with candles extinguished by force of air.

# AWFUL DEATHS

## AS SEVEN MEN MEET THEIR DOOM BY DROWNING IN SLIME

### THE MINERS LOST FOREVER WERE:

## SINCOCK, CHING, PENALUNA, ANDREW, two DUNSTANS and COMBLEDICK

Now that their time on earth is over and at the gates they stand. Those prepared shall be seen standing at GOD'S right hand.

Fig. 6.   The hazards of mining, reflected in these headlines of 1858.

ceased operation. Tin mining, though, was beginning to benefit from continental influences, particularly the expertise of German engineers whose experience of shaft mining and pumping technology was far superior to that of their rather conservative Cornish counterparts. The initiative to import foreign expertise came from a small band of entrepreneurial landowners such as Sir Francis Godolphin and William Carnsew, whose willingness to open new speculative ventures was to play an increasingly important rôle in the modernisation and expansion of the Cornish industry. While the financial risks were high for these 'adventurers', there was nevertheless the very real possibility that a lucky strike could transform the fortunes of modest landowning families and secure their elevation to the senior ranks of the west-country gentry.

The increasing capitalisation of the mining industry in the 16th and 17th centuries also diversified its organisational structure. The small concern of a single miner, perhaps with a few hired labourers, working his own claim continued, but became progressively overshadowed by corporate concerns as operational costs became too high, as Carew put it, 'for any one man's purse'. Small partnerships, in which costs and profits were shared, were becoming more common, some adopting the cost-agreement system by which some partners did not actually work themselves but hired substitutes to perform their share of the labour. During the course of the 17th century both these models came to be dwarfed by the tribute system, by which a mine was leased from its owner, often backed by other shareholders, in return for a fixed share of the profits. Such concerns were in the charge of mine captains who administered the daily operations and were often held in high esteem by the landowners and labourers alike.

In 1700 copper production stood at *c.* 1500 tons, rising substantially once Newcomen's Beam Engine was introduced into the county in the early 1740s, which enabled deeper lodes to be worked. By the end of the century further advances in the removal of water had been made by James Watt and Richard Trevithick, and their improved steam engines had become common throughout the principal mining regions of St Just, Hensbarrow, Redruth, Bodmin Moor and the Tamar valley. Between 1740 and 1775 the number of copper-producing units trebled and by 1856, despite periodic slumps, copper production had soared to 209,000 tons, much of it despatched to South Wales from the little ports of Hayle, Portreath and Morwellham. Tin, although popularly thought to have been the mainstay of Cornish mining, was running a poor second with an annual output of only 100,000 tons.

Mining, particularly in its later stages, was a hazardous occupation and the outside world was occasionally reminded of the fact, as in 1846 when 39 men perished at Wheal Rose when the mine flooded. One late 18th-century traveller, having satisfied his curiosity to be taken down to the main workings, wrote, 'had I known what we should endure, I never should have attempted it'. He described the picture encountered

*Richard Trevithick*

95

# AN ADDRESS
## From the Mayor & Magistrates of Helston, and the Magistrates of the West Division of Kirrier, to the
# MINERS
# AND LABOURING CLASSES

The Mayor and Magistrates of Helston, and the Magistrates acting for the West Division of the Hundred of Kirrier, express their sincere regret and concern at the present high price of the necessaries of life, which occasions so much Distress amongst the Miners and other Labourers.

They have already endeavoured to lessen this distress by raising Money in several Parishes, and providing Flour and other Food for those who were most in want of such aid.

It is also their intention to take such further measures as shall lessen the sufferings of the labouring classes, but nothing they can do can altogether remove the evil, till it shall please Providence to give a cheaper supply of Food.

But they must at the same time exhort the people to bear their distress with patience, and they trust to the good feeling of the Cornish Miners not to allow their distress, or their discontent, or the persuasions of the ill-disposed to urge them on to acts of violence, which will do them no good, but will compel the Magistates to put in force those powers which the Law has given them, for they have sufficient means placed at their disposal to repress acts of violence and to punish the wrong doers.

The Mayor and Magistrates therefore exhort you to return quietly to your own homes, & to trust to your friends & Neighbours to adopt such measures as are most likely to lessen the present distress, which any acts of violence on your part can only tend to increase.

**FRANCIS JAMES, Mayor.**

**JOHN KENDALL, Justice for Helston.**

| | | |
|---|---|---|
| **JOHN ROGERS,** | **C. W. POPHAM,** | Justices for the West |
| **JOHN PETER,** | **W. THOMAS.** | Division of Kirrier, |

Fig. 7. Pleas for calm from the local magistrates, like this example from Helston, were often necessary to restrain the working classes during times of economic depression.

37. The once familiar 'Cornish Riviera' express carried countless holidaymakers to the duchy between the wars.

38. Calstock viaduct.

39.  Porthminster Beach, St Ives.

40.  Western Beach, Newquay, at the turn of the century.

41. Fashionably-dressed ladies on the promenade at Penzance in 1900.

42.  Truro Cathedral: the building of the Nave and West End.

at a depth of 500 feet, 'where some poor creatures were busied in the process of their miserable employment, with hardly room to move their bodies, in sulpherous air, wet to the skin, and buried in the solid rock, these, our fellow mortals, live and work for their daily bread'. If conditions underground were atrocious, then wages were little comfort with few miners earning more than 13s. 0d. (65 p) a week, and many considerably less. For most, however, including the 'bal maidens' who worked at the surface, there was little alternative, and the harshness of the 1834 Poor Law Act, which abolished assistance to the able-bodied unless they entered the hated workhouses or 'bastilles' as they were commonly known, condemned thousands to a fate 'in the bowels of the earth'.

*Penzance-born Sir Humphry Davy*

The enhanced employment opportunities offered by the expansion of mining had, in the meantime, contributed to a population boom. Throughout the 18th century Cornwall's population had risen steadily, from an estimated 106,000 in 1700 to 192,281, according to the first official census of 1801. Within the following 60 years, however, the total almost doubled again to reach 362,343 in 1861. For many localities this meant the rapid transformation of hamlets into towns within the lifetime of two generations; in 1801 the parish of St Cleer near Caradon had a population of 774, in 1831 the figure stood at 982, but then came the discovery of copper, and by 1861 the total had almost reached 4,000. By 1921, on the other hand, the county's total had actually fallen by some 42,000, or 12 per cent, when the population of England and Wales as a whole had risen by a further 88 per cent. In other words, an equivalent increase should have pushed the Cornish population to something in the region of 680,000. The explanation behind this later decline is not difficult to find, and we would only have to look among the surnames in the telephone directories of New South Wales, Wisconsin, Nevada, Michigan, the Transvaal as well as a host of British towns for the answer. People had become one of Cornwall's leading exports.

Emigration from the county had begun on a small scale in the early 18th century and there are references to the Cornish language being heard in North America in the 1750s. The expertise of Cornish miners and mining engineers was being welcomed in Chile, Peru and Canada, while at Rio del Monto in Mexico the authorities still maintain their separate Cornish cemetery, where gravestones from the 1820s record the names of scores of Cornish silver adventurers, Pengellys, Hoskins, Scuses and Williams, victims of disease and the elusive search for a better life. The agricultural depression of the 1840s contributed to a gradual acceleration, and by the mid 1860s the steady trickle was developing into a flood. The price of copper and tin was falling dramatically as foreign competitors, with their reduced labour costs, were forcing Cornwall from the world markets. Years of inadequate investment on the part of the mine owners now took its toll and the domestic industry was on the verge of a rapid demise. In 1866 alone, about

# EMIGRATION
## TO
# *SOUTH*
# AUSTRALIA

Her Majesty's Colonization Commissioners having determined to dispatch in the course of a few weeks a large number of Emigrants, all eligible persons may obtain, by making an IMMEDIATE application, a

# FREE
# PASSAGE!

*The classes of persons now in requisition are*
## Agricultural Laborers,
## SHEPHERDS, CARPENTERS
# BLACKSMITHS
### AND
## *STONE MASONS*
### And all Persons connected with Building.
*Application to be made to*
# Mr. L LATIMER,
## *Rosewin-row, TRURO.*

E. MEARD, PRINTER AND BOOKBINDER, BOSCAWEN-STREET, TRURO.

Fig. 9. During the late 19th century the contraction of the Cornish economy prompted thousands to respond to emigration opportunities like this example from Truro.

twenty Cornish mines closed down and 5,000 miners emigrated. For those still working, wages had also fallen from about 16s. 0d. (80 p) to 11s. 0d. (55 p) a week, and many families were forced to fall back on the parish and the workhouse. The following year, 1867, was even worse and a further 11,000 miners lost their jobs, of whom some two-thirds chose to emigrate rather than face a bleak existence on the Poor Law. Others delayed the inevitable decision for another year or two in the hope that things might improve. The continued retraction of copper mining, however, with the number of mines falling from 174 in 1864 to 80 by 1870, plus a 50 per cent fall in the price of tin between 1872-8, meant that the decision was made for them. Between 1871-81 Cornwall's population fell by a further nine per cent, and the mining population by a staggering 24 per cent. Nearly 9,000 left the Penzance area alone during the course of the decade.

Naturally enough, these emigrants were mainly attracted to other mining areas where their skills could be put to good use, and such was the scale of the exodus that one traveller was soon able to make the well-known observation that 'wherever a hole is sunk in the ground, you will be sure to find a Cornishman at the bottom of it'. The lead mines of Wisconsin, the copper mines of Montana, the coalfields of Pennsylvania, the gold and silver mines of Colorado and California were all powerful magnets, and by the First World War about 100,000 Cornish folk had settled in the U.S.A. alone. There they were given the nickname of 'Cousin Jacks', a term which has become synonymous with 'Cornishman' ever since, and which is said to have originated when nearly every Cornish miner, when asked if he knew of a good worker to fill a particular job, would invariably answer that he would 'send 'ome fer cousin Jack'.

If the majority of Cornish emigrants settled in North America, there were many other countries with their holes in the ground which also attracted substantial numbers. In 1870 there were 85 Cornishmen at the Tocapilla mine in Brazil, and thousands more in Australia, including the fearless crew of the 36 ft. lugger *Mystery* which had sailed all the way from Mount's Bay in 1854, a journey which took 116 days. Nor should we forget those who settled in other parts of the United Kingdom. Wales, geographically convenient and with rich mineral deposits, had been an early attraction, and Cornishmen could be found working in the Neath smelting industry as early as the 1580s. The development of the Anglesey copper mines at the beginning of the 19th century attracted a later wave of migrants, and some, like James Treweek of Gwennap, became well-known figures. Henry Dennis, who moved to Denbighshire *c.* 1850, was another who entered the ranks of Welsh society, building up an industrial empire which eventually had 10,000 employees. On the whole, however, it was not North Wales which attracted the greatest number of Cornish workers, but the developing industrial valleys of Glamorgan and west Monmouthshire. According to the 1851 census, there were already 756 Cornish people in Swansea

*Billy Bray, preacher and miner*

99

alone, and the economic decline of the latter half of the century prompted many thousands to join them. The industrial towns of England also attracted their share, while hundreds of others moved up to the new ironfields of Cumberland. Work was also to be found in Scotland, and in a single year, 1866, some 1,500 Cornish miners left for the collieries of Ayrshire and Lanarkshire.

The scale of this exodus had serious repercussions for the society left behind. Although many who left would eventually send for their families to join them, the immediate consequence was a social structure deprived of much of its manhood, vitality and supportive capacity. Thousands of wives, children and old people, receiving only occasional remittances from abroad, were left to survive on handouts from the poor relief funds, and in 1867 there were no less than 1,413 claimants in the single mining parish of St Just, all forced to exist on 1s. 1d. (7p) a week. Cultural and sporting life also suffered accordingly, and it was becoming more common to find an exhibition of Cornish wrestling in the mining camps of Butte, Montana, than at home.

Tragic the story may be — and the romanticist might well consider the consequences for today if there had been no syphoning-off and Cornwall's population stood at about one million — the picture would have been much worse were it not for the late 19th-century growth of other employment opportunities. The expansion of drift fishing saved many potential 'Cousin Jacks' from joining their relatives overseas, while an increase in China clay working also helped keep several thousand mid-Cornwall copper miners at home. China clay takes its name from the Chinese method of using kaolin, a derivative of granite, to manufacture porcelain. The Chinese had managed to guard the secrets of the production process until the early 18th century, but their technology was leaked to the West and in 1746 kaolin was discovered in the St Austell area. During the early days of the industry, clay working was looked upon as inferior to mining proper and by 1810 there were only seven small workings in operation. The crisis in the copper mines, however, forced many to abandon their prejudices and by 1857 the St Austell clay works employed about 1,700 men with an annual output of 68,000 tons. By 1867 the workforce had increased to 4,000, production to 160,000 tons and an important diversification of the Cornish economy had been achieved.

Despite a history of fluctuating fortunes, Cornish agriculture, long the Cinderella of local industry, was also in a fairly healthy state, at least compared with the slump periods of the 1840s and early 1850s. In his *Memoirs* Jonathan Couch of Polperro blamed the repeal of the Corn Laws in 1846 which opened the door to foreign corn entering the domestic market, complaining that landlords had been forced to reduce rents by an average of 25 per cent. Even then, he added, it was hard to find new tenants as many farmers were emigrating to America. The arrival of the mainline railway in 1859, however, proved a crucial lifeline for the agricultural as well as the fishing communities. Small

*Early industrial railway engine from the Tamar valley*

100

branch lines had been built in the county since 1837 but with the completion of Brunel's bridge across the Tamar came new opportunities. Within three years over 2,000 tons of fish and early potatoes were despatched each year to the industrial towns hungry for fresh produce. The farmers were not slow, ever, to satisfy the growing Victorian demand for daffodils, violets and anemones, and by the end of the century over 500 tons of flowers left the county annually. Cornwall's mild climate was admirably suited to the growing of early vegetables, and by 1890 over 3,000 tons of spring cabbage and broccoli were carried annually by train to Covent Garden and other centres.

*Brunel's bridge across the Tamar*

If the rapid collapse of the copper industry had taken its toll on many parts of the county, particularly the central areas, the more protracted death of tin mining saved the souls of many communities in the western parishes. Although tin prices had fallen sharply and many tinners had also been forced to emigrate, thousands of other families were able to remain and eke out a living as the industry slowly approached its demise. The mines at Balleswidden and Ding Dong had closed in the 1870s, but Wheal Owles survived until 1893 and Botallack for another four years. A score of others, mainly in the St Ives, Pendeen, Wendron and Camborne areas, struggled into the 20th century before finally going under.

Fig. 10. An early print of a small-scale tin mine with the 'bal maidens' at work, breaking down the ore.

# XII Society, Religion and Politics in the Nineteenth Century

*Cannon, formerly at Falmouth, from the* Bellerophon *which brought Napoleon to England*

As the 18th century drew to its close Cornwall still remained one of the remotest areas of the kingdom. Roads were primitive, 'the worst in all England', complained one traveller, while there was little familiarity with wider national or international affairs before the first county newspaper began in 1801. The accounts of smuggling and wrecking clearly point to a fairly widespread disrespect for the law, and the rather contemptuous observations of several up-country travellers indicate that the Cornish were generally thought of as uncouth barbarians, steeped in superstition and more pagan than Christian. One Penzance businessman complained in 1803 that whenever he visited London he met with the preconceived view that in Cornwall 'the underground inhabitants (piskeys) are the most numerous ... the above-ground gentlemen are called smugglers ... those who are not stone-eaters are cannabils'. If the Cornish language had finally expired, the particular version of spoken English which replaced it was still a hurdle to be surmounted, James Forbes noting that 'it requires some attention to understand the miners and the lower classes of the people'. Other visitors were disdainful of some of the social habits, complaining, for example, that 'both men, women and children have all their pipes of tobacco in their mouths and soe sit round the fire smoking', while the local gentry were often no more complimentary. To Edward Giddy of Tredrea near Marazion, his neighbours were prone to 'perjury, drunkeness, idleness, poverty, contempt of the law, and a universal corruption of manners'.

It was easy, though, to make such criticisms from the relative comfort of the local manor house since the living conditions of the labouring classes were hardly conducive to fostering the niceties of social etiquette. In his *Survey* of 1602 Richard Carew wrote of a general improvement in the housing stock during his lifetime, and yet there remains considerable evidence to the contrary, at least in the central and western parts of the county. The dwellings of the tinners and farm labourers were normally self-built, on land rented for a period of three lives, and were accordingly fairly primitive. The descriptions provided by writers like William Bottrell have much more recently been largely substantiated by the results of archaeological enquiry. Within the Iron Age village of Carn Euny in Penwith a cottage of *c*. 1750 was excavated in 1968 and the findings were in general agreement with those derived from other examples in the far west and the Lizard. The rectangular

*Silver shoulder-belt of the Cornish yeomanry at the time of Napoleon*

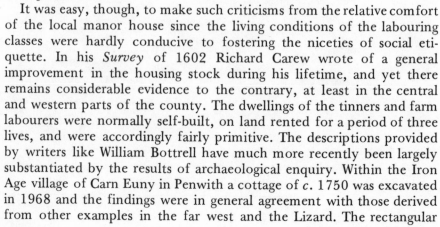

granite-built cottage measured 11 ft. 6 ins. (3.5 m) by 23 ft. (7 m) and probably had an upper storey reached by ladder with a thatched roof. Traces of a wooden partition suggested that the building was divided into two nearly equal rooms with the interior lime-washed and the floor composed of 'rab', subsoil mixed with water. A large inglenook fireplace stood at the western end and cooking was probably done over an open hearth. Another, later, example from the Scillies indicated that an even more basic type of dwelling continued in use in such remote areas where building materials were limited. In 1977 Howard Mason led a team of archaeologists to the island of Samson and excavated a single-roomed dwelling, similar in dimensions to the Carn Euny example, which was occupied *c.* 1833-55. Detailed finds included pottery fragments, brass buttons, gun flints, and pieces of clay pipes, while the main ingredient of the inhabitants' diet was indicated by a midden of no less than 100,000 limpet shells.

*A clay pipe from Samson, Isles of Scilly*

If living conditions were poor, wages were little better. At the beginning of the 19th century farm labourers earned about 6s. 0d. to 9s. 0d. (30-45 p) a week, miners and fishermen a little more but on an irregular basis. With beef a rarity and poultry costing upwards of a day's pay, meat was not a regular feature of the average household diet, except when the time came to slaughter the familiar household pig, 'the gentleman that earns his rent'. Fortunately, fresh fish was plentiful and cheap, especially pilchards, while Forbes commented in 1794 on the availability of 'the finest cod, ling . . . at less than 1$^d$ per lb'. There was, of course, the humble but celebrated pasty to fall back on, the same writer noting that 'the poor have a method of making pasties . . . of substantial crust, and when baked will keep a good long time. These pasties the labourers take into the fields and the miners to their works, and seem to regale on them with high glee'.

For the average labouring family disease, epidemics and a high rate of infant mortality were realities which had to be regularly faced. The great cholera epidemic of 1831 reached Cornwall in August of that year, probably brought by mariners and fishermen since the ports of Padstow, Hayle and Newlyn were the worst hit. By December the single parish of Paul had buried 88 victims, and villagers were forced to impose quarantines on their neighbours. Those who survived had little prospect of a long life and, as the 19th century progressed, overcrowding and insanitary living conditions made matters worse. Between 1813-30 almost 20 per cent of burials at St Cleer were of children under five, but by the late 1850s the proportion had risen to over half. Life expectancy fell dramatically, particularly in the mining areas, and the 600 males buried at St Just during the 1840s had an average age of only 25 years and eight months. At St Cleer again, the average age of interments dropped dramatically from 51 in 1819 to under 22 by 1860.

There was little immediate prospect, either, of a political solution to this deprivation. A severely restricted franchise and a property qualification which allowed only the wealthy to become M.P.s produced a

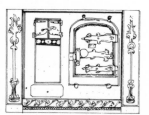

*A Cornish cooking range*

House of Commons which was unrepresentative of the masses and largely uncaring of their plight. Cornish politics, in any case, was a den of corruption into which notions of democracy did not enter. National labels of Whig and Tory meant little in a county in which the local landed gentry, aided by an archaic system of election and representation, determined which candidates were returned to Parliament. In the first place, Cornwall was grossly over-represented in the Commons. Each of the 21 boroughs returned two members apiece to supplement the standard county allocation of a further two M.P.s, although the latter seats were rarely contested as candidates were normally returned unopposed. Such elections as did take place in the boroughs involved only a small number of voters, less than 1,400 in 1760, and in a system of open voting the local aristocracy generally determined the outcome. Cornwall, in fact, was notorious for its 'rotten boroughs' in which voters sold their preferences to the highest bidder. In 1740 Thomas Pitt had reported that 'there are few [Cornish] boroughs where the common sort of people do not think they have as much right to sell themselves and their votes, as they have to sell their corn and their cattle'. Seven years later, in an attempt to secure Grampound, Pitt despairingly reported to his leaders that 'we can carry it, but it must cost damnably dear. The villains . . . rise in their demands so extravagantly, that I have been very near damning them . . . the dirty rascals despise 20 guineas'. Others could expect even more; the 40 voters at Camelford were demanding up to £300 each, while an even greater price could be obtained by the electors of Mitchell in 1829 who numbered precisely seven! In most boroughs, however, the hold of the landed gentry was so strong that a contest was hardly necessary. From the reign of Edward II to the Reform Act of 1832 no less than 23 members of the Trelawney family represented Looe in the Commons, while Penryn was firmly in the hands of Lord Edgecumbe and Lord Falmouth. Fowey, with less than 100 voters, was a pocket borough of the Rashleigh family, Callington likewise in the grip of Lady Orford. Even when an outside candidate was prepared to make a challenge, as happened at Penryn in 1765, the bias of the returning officer ensured defeat by manipulating the voting figures in favour of Philip Rashleigh. It was only in a handful of boroughs, in fact, that an 'independent' candidate could expect much of a chance and, apart from Bossiney, Tregony and Grampound, most seats were not worth the expense of contesting.

Pressure to reform this archaic system had been gradually growing since John Wilkes in the 1760s, and the movement gained momentum from the dissemination of radical ideas which followed the French Revolution. Individual M.P.s, however, could hardly be expected to abandon a system which worked in their interests and, apart from a few cosmetic modifications including the disenfranchisement of Grampound in 1821, there was no marked change until the Reform Act of 1832. This nationally modest measure was justifiably harsh on

104

43. (*above*) Recruiting march in East Street, Newquay, *c.* 1914.

44. (*below*) H.M. Airship C9 at Mullion harbour after damage on a long patrol to Jersey, 23 July 1916.

45. (*above*) Broad Street, Launceston.
46. (*below*) Street scene, Camborne.

47. (*above*) Gorran Haven.
48. (*below*) Lands End.

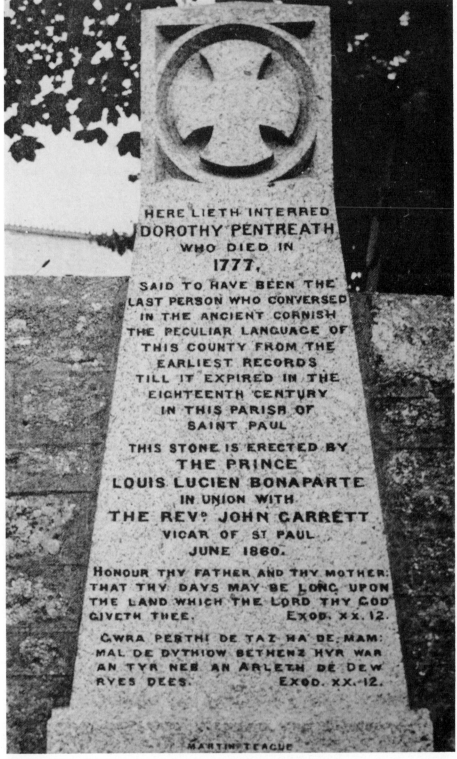

HERE LIETH INTERRED
DOROTHY PENTREATH
WHO DIED IN
1777,
SAID TO HAVE BEEN THE
LAST PERSON WHO CONVERSED
IN THE ANCIENT CORNISH
THE PECULIAR LANGUAGE OF
THIS COUNTY FROM THE
EARLIEST RECORDS
TILL IT EXPIRED IN THE
EIGHTEENTH CENTURY
IN THIS PARISH OF
SAINT PAUL

THIS STONE IS ERECTED BY
THE PRINCE
LOUIS LUCIEN BONAPARTE
IN UNION WITH
THE REV? JOHN GARRETT
VICAR OF S? PAUL
JUNE 1860.

HONOUR THY FATHER AND THY MOTHER:
THAT THY DAYS MAY BE LONG UPON
THE LAND WHICH THE LORD THY GOD
GIVETH THEE.          EXOD. XX. 12.

GWRA PERTHI DE TAZ HA DE MAM:
MAL DE DYTHIOW BETHENZ HYR WAR
AN TYR NEB AN ARLETH DE DEW
RYES DEES.          EXOD. XX. 12.

MARTIN TEAGUE

49.  Symbol of a lost age: the memorial at Paul to Dolly Pentreath, last native speaker
of the Cornish language.

Cornwall, reducing her representation to 12, two dual-member County seats, East and West, plus separate representation for Helston, Liskeard, Launceston and St Ives (one member each) and two members for Truro and Penryn-with-Falmouth. The total electorate, however, remained small and over 80 per cent of adult males were left below the voting qualification. Uncontested elections remained the norm especially in the County seats, where Cornwall West saw no contest at all until after the Second Reform Act of 1867, and Cornwall East only three.

*John Wesley caught in a storm off St Ives*

It was to this world of inadequate representation, corruption, lawlessness and poverty that Methodism at least offered a spiritual solution. The Methodist movement, part of the so-called 'New Dissent', had grown up as a reaction to the irreligious climate of the early 18th century when the pace of scientific and philosophical advance seemed to be making theology dispensable. At the same time the established church, the Church of England, had largely lost its ability to launch a counter-offensive and was proving unable to adapt to the changing intellectual and economic climate of the day. Its cumbersome bureaucratic structure prevented the introduction of a comprehensive programme of new church building, desperately needed both to keep up with changing population patterns and to cater for the growing industrial communities. As a result, Anglicanism had become weakest in large, rural parishes with a dispersed population, which were experiencing substantial social change through the increase in industrial activity. Pluralism was also rife as the low income of many parishes forced the clergy to take on several livings, leaving the congregations poorly served in the process. In 1748 the western parishes of St Ives, Lelant, Zennor and Towednack were all in the hands of one incumbent, and such was the neglect that the dead were being left a fortnight before burial services could be arranged.

Against this background John Wesley set out to restore heart religion and evangelism among the masses, to save souls and correct moral laxity, and from its small beginnings in 1738 Methodism grew rapidly, although not without resistance. Wesley himself was struck on the head while preaching at St Ives in 1745, and in the following year one of his prominent followers, James Wheatley, was attacked by a West Cornwall mob and only saved from death by the intervention of the mayor who was forced to read the Riot Act. Despite the opposition of conventional Anglicanism, however, the new movement was taking root and in 1747 the vicar of Lelant was complaining that in St Ives 'there are likewise many people . . . called methodists who frequently assemble at the house of John Nance at unreasonable hours'.

It would be quite wrong, though, to view the growth of Methodism in Cornwall or, indeed, anywhere else in terms of a steady and uninterrupted advance. Apart from the vociferous opposition of much of the establishment, the very nature of the movement, at least in its early days, did not lend itself easily to mass membership. Local methodists were organised into societies which were then subdivided into small

*An early Methodist chapel*

classes of about five to twelve members who paid 1d. a week towards the cost of a meeting-place. This intimate structure and the almost puritanical nature of the movement proved too much for many, and several societies had very chequered histories. At Launceston in 1760 Wesley found 'the small remains of a dead, scattered society: and no wonder, as they have scarce any discipline, and only one sermon in a fortnight'. Two years later, however, he preached his first of many sermons in the famous Gwennap Pit near Redruth and, by 1781, at the age of 78, he was attracting a crowd of over 20,000 people. By the end of the century Methodism had become firmly rooted in Cornwall, and in 1794, three years after the founder's death, James Forbes noted 'the portrait of the celebrated John Wesley in many of the poor houses in Cornwall, where his memory is held in veneration and his labours were frequently blessed'.

Methodism's appeal, as Forbes implies, was greatest among the working classes, farm labourers and fishermen, while even the notorious hard-drinking tinners were being won over, the arch-opponent the Revd. Sydney Smith complaining in 1807 that 'all mines and subterranean places belong to them'. While this was perhaps an exaggeration, hundreds of little chapels appeared throughout the length and breadth of the county, evoking not only a renewed spirit of religion but a new sense of morality and communal life. The advance of Methodism by mid-century is clear from the great Religious Census of 1851 which revealed that over 60 per cent of Cornish churchgoers subscribed to it and only 27 per cent were Anglican. The remainder were mainly Independents and Baptists while the county's pitifully small number of Catholics, 0.4 per cent, was the second lowest in England. The growth of Methodism not only provoked the antagonism of the Church of England but inevitably increased resentment over the vexed issue of the tithe. While it was true that the mechanics of tithe collection had become largely divorced from things religious and had passed into the hands of lay speculators, an association with the established church remained firmly planted in the minds of the people. Many were increasingly refusing to pay, especially the fishermen who were proving to be the vanguard of resistance. In 1830, for example, the by now predominantly Methodist fishermen of Newlyn and Mousehole refused to comply, attacked the bailiff sent to enforce a writ on them, and so terrified the tithe owners that they won the right of exemption.

While there are other instances of militant opposition to the tithe, it would be wrong to interpret this resistance as a symptom of the kind of political radicalism which characterised the Welsh 'tithe wars' during the second half of the century. On the contrary, the increasing association between nonconformity and radicalism which was being formulated in many other areas, the industrialised North and Midlands as well as Wales, was not echoed in Cornwall. For one thing, the particular version of nonconformity espoused by the Cornish did not encourage political action. The Marxist historian Eric Hobsbawm has claimed that

'Methodism in Cornwall produced an atmosphere of resignation and acceptance which worked against militancy' and, while this may be an over-simplification, it remains the case that Wesley himself had been opposed to the involvement of his supporters in political activities, a view not shared by the Primitive Methodists, expelled in 1812, or by the United Free Methodists who broke away from the parent body in 1849. It may have been a Cornishman, William Lovett of Newlyn, who helped found the Chartist movement with its demands for universal adult male suffrage and a major reform of the whole representation and electoral system, but his campaign met with a mixed response from his own people. When one of his organisers visited St Ives in 1839 and asked if there were any Chartists about, he was informed that 'they catch no fish here but pilchards and mackerel'! Several local Chartist societies were founded and flourished for a while, one follower was even elected to Penzance Town Council, but overall the Cornish showed only a passing interest. In fact, apart from a series of unco-ordinated food riots during the 1840s, mainly by the notoriously lawless tinners, there are few indications of working class political activity.

*James Polkinghorne, famous wrestler*

The Methodist promise of a decent after-life may have reduced the desire to improve the earthly one, and the old adage that poverty was 'the wages of sin' led many to accept divine judgement as the explanation for their place in the social order. There were other, however, non-religious factors at work in the formation of the county's political character. To begin with, the structure and organisation of the main occupations worked against the fostering of radicalism and class unity. In the fishing industry a trend towards a share-payment was becoming increasingly common as drifting replaced seining, and this resulted in fierce competition and greater emphasis on individual enterprise. Neither did the organisational nature and salary arrangements in the mines contribute to the kind of political consciousness which characterised the coal and steel industries.

Evidence from the medieval period shows a tendency towards small unit workings with tinning rarely a full-time occupation. The expansion of the industry in the 18th and 19th centuries was characterised by the growth of the tribute system by which groups of miners known as *pares* competed against each other by bidding for working areas or *pitches*, and paid a percentage of the value of the ore won to the mine owners. The lesser skilled tutworkers, who dug the shafts and prepared the levels, were also paid per completed fathom, and all this emphasis on individual effort was not conducive to fostering the kind of working-class consciousness which developed in other industrial areas of Britain. This is clearly reflected in the failure of trade unionism to take root in 19th-century Cornwall and, apart from an unsuccessful strike in 1866 and the formation of a short-lived Miners Association, there were few concerted attempts to unify the workforce. Cornish miners, in any case, were geographically isolated from other mining areas, and the power of the local landowners remained a potent factor throughout the industry's lifetime.

The combined effect of all these factors was the moulding of an essentially moderate, highly individualistic and sometimes passive political mentality which often frustrated activists. One Chartist organiser desperately reported that 'you can have no conception of the ignorance of the people upon general politics', while another was even less complimentary, complaining that the population 'were slaves to the aristocracy and the moneyocracy'. By the later decades of the century, when the Unitarians, Independents and Baptists had turned the Welsh into a nation of radicals, the Cornish remained aloof, and any connotations of solidarity suggested by the county motto of 'One and All' were distinctly absent from the ranks of the Cornish working class. The general election returns from the 1880s and 1890s endorse these conclusions. The Reform Act of 1884–5 reduced the number of Cornish seats from 12 to six, but also extended the franchise to a majority of adult males. The great political issue of the day was Gladstone's attempts to push through Irish Home Rule, despite the opposition not only of the Conservatives but a sizeable number of his own party led by Joseph Chamberlain. The controversy was enough to split the Liberals; Chamberlain broke away to form his Liberal-Unionist party with its strong imperialistic overtones, and established an electoral pact with the Tories, hence the complete absence of Tory M.P.s from all Cornish seats between 1885 and 1910. Home Rule was vigorously opposed by the conservative Wesleyans, and while many Liberal-Unionist candidates elsewhere took a thrashing, they were so successful in Cornwall that the county became known as 'Chamberlain's Duchy'. The farmers, in particular, swung heavily away from the mainstream Liberals with devastating results at the polls, and it is clear that Gladstone's progressive stance was popular only in the mining and clay-working seats of Mid and North-East Cornwall. The eventual merger between Liberal-Unionism and Conservatism, largely completed by the end of the century, was in Cornwall a subconscious reality well before it became a formal political one.

# XIII  The Twentieth Century

*The Cornish flag of St Piran*

The decline of Cornwall's staple industries, which had been a feature of the last quarter of the 19th century, continued into the twentieth. Mining, in particular, continued to contract and the disruptive effect of the First World War on the world economy was all too clearly felt by the county's remaining tinners. In 1920 Cornwall produced 3,065 tons of black tin but in the early months of 1921 the market price fell by half and output slumped catastrophically to 679 tons. Operations came to a halt at the leading concerns of Geevor, Lelant and South Crofty and, with only a handful of smaller mines still working, a mere 370 tons was produced in 1922. There were still, however, a few undaunted adventurers prepared to keep going, particularly in the Wendron area to the north of Helston. East Lovell and Wheal Enys continued for a few more years and Calvadnack mine until 1930. Even the occasional new enterprise was started, like Polhigey mine which began operations in 1926 and was later visited by the Prince of Wales. In general, though, world economic conditions dictated that, if mining was to survive in Cornwall where unit costs were high, it could only be through rationalisation and capitalisation with investment concentrated in a small number of the most productive concerns.

The contraction in the mining industry and the social disruption which followed was to a large extent echoed by the demise of fishing. The expansion of pilchard and mackerel drifting during the 1880s and 1890s had brought obvious benefits to Cornwall's coastal communities, but the increasing mobility of the national fishing fleet was now bringing a marked increase in the number of East Coast vessels working Cornish waters. As these larger steam drifters took an ever-larger share of the catch, tension gradually increased and the Newlyn Riots of 1896, ostensibly over the 'Yorkies' reluctance to observe the Sabbath, had already revealed the depth of local frustration aroused by over-fishing and fanned by regional rivalry. A crisis point in the industry was reached in 1905 when catches greatly exceeded market demands and huge quantities of pilchards were either dumped or sold to farmers for manure at giveaway prices. This precipitated a sharp slump as hundreds of fishermen abandoned their calling for other occupations, many leaving the county in the process. The inter-war period continued to witness a progressive decline, the County Fishery Officer described the 1930 season as 'an utter failure', and full-time fishing virtually disappeared from many of the smaller coves and harbours; even the

109

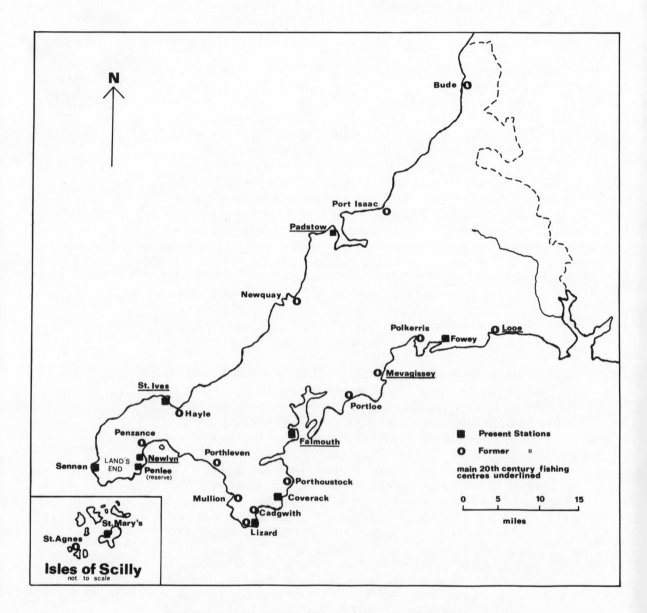

Maritime Cornwall, showing lifeboat stations and fishing centres.

established ports saw their fleets decimated. Mousehole's comple-
ment of 100 drifters had disappeared by the 1940s, while on the
opposite side of Mount's Bay Porthleven's fleet of 128 working boats
in 1897 had shrunk by 26 by 1957. Inevitably this contraction was
characterised by a disruption of community life as many families
moved out and ancillary trades laid off workers, a process aggravated
by a government policy of so-called 'slum clearance' laid down in the
Housing Acts of 1930-5. Although primarily intended to alleviate
conditions in the inner cities, the legislation empowered all local
authorities to participate, and the policy led to the demolition of many
of the old fishermen's quarters. In October 1937 the men of Newlyn
sailed the *Rosebud* the 460 miles to London to protest 'against the
wholesale destruction of our village', but, despite a ministerial audience
and mass public attention and sympathy, they managed only a partial
victory. Fishermen, perhaps like Cornwall itself, were becoming peripheral to 'national' considerations.

The economic contraction of the 1920s and 1930s was followed by
the disruptive effects of the Second World War. The Great War of
1914-18 had not been directly felt in Cornwall beyond a modest
amount of German submarine activity in coastal waters, but the countless war memorials scattered throughout the peninsula indicate that the
county had given its 'lost generation' like everywhere else. While
Plymouth was to bear the brunt of the Luftwaffe's *blitzkrieg* in the
south-west, Cornwall was not allowed to escape from the consequences
of curtailing German nationalism a second time. Ports and harbours
were inevitable targets; an air raid on Penryn in May 1941 destroyed 23
houses, a shop and the Church Institute, while another on 6 September
damaged 13 houses beyond repair. Penzance was also bombed on
several occasions, and between 1940-2 the town lost 48 dwellings with
16 fatalities. Fishermen played an important part in the Dunkirk
evacuation of June 1940 in an atmosphere of great secrecy. Boats
returning from sea were simply instructed to remove their nets, take on
fuel, and sail immediately to Falmouth to await further orders. Provision was made for Hitler's anticipated invasion just as it had been for
Napoleon's a century and a half earlier. The Cornwall County Defence
Committee was set up to make the necessary preparations, although
it was probably just as well that the inhabitants were unaware of the
government's private conclusion that, if invaded, Cornwall would
probably have to be abandoned to the enemy. Fortunately Hitler's
'Operation Sealion' failed to materialise, and on the whole the county
escaped lightly, and assumed the ancillary rôle of catering for evacuees
from the cities as well as refugees from France and Belgium.

*An early view of the
Market Hall, Penzance*

While the war provided a temporary boost to the local economy,
Cornwall's traditional industries remained highly vulnerable. Fishing
was good during the late 1940s after grounds had been rested during
the war and stocks had increased, but the industry soon had to meet
the challenge of the more advanced continental fleets. Considerable

*The Penlee lifeboat*
Solomon Browne, *lost*
*with all hands in*
*December 1981*

capital investment was also needed to counteract the final demise of pilchard drifting and to switch to other methods and species. In 1947 there had still been 600 drifters employing 3,500 men, but by 1967 only 10 boats and 56 men were left. The 1959 Sea Fisheries Act attempted to stop the rot by introducing government subsidies but, beneficial as it was, the legislation did not cover shellfish, an omission which caused the County Fishery Officer to 'express his astonishment'. It was to be mother nature, however, not government action, which provided a lifeline for Cornwall's remaining 2,000 fishermen with the arrival of large shoals of winter mackerel in the late 1960s. While the bonanza proved to be relatively short-lived, the injection of confidence stimulated modernisation of the fleet with greater emphasis on versatility. The recent development at the main ports of Newlyn and Falmouth, with improved berthing and service facilities, has ensured the survival of one of the county's oldest pursuits, even if it still remains a precarious and unpredictable occupation.

The fluctuating fortunes in the fishing industry were also echoed in the mining areas. The catastrophic fall in world tin prices during the early 1920s led many to predict the complete demise of the industry as several more concerns ceased production. With the closure of the great Levant workings in 1930 and East Pool and Wheal Agar in 1945, mineral extraction in Cornwall seemed to be entering a terminal phase but, like fishing, tin mining underwent rationalisation with investment concentrated in a small number of viable concerns such as Geevor, Wheal Jane, Mount Wellington, South Crofty and Pendarves. In 1969 a writer in *The Observer* predicted that the Cornish industry faced a 'considerable renaissance' but, with high production and labour costs, tin mining has always been vulnerable to the vagaries of the world market; a slump in ore prices in 1978 led to the closure of Mount Wellington and Wheal Jane. The latter reopened a year later, and improved prospects saw the birth of a new venture, Wheal Concorde near Redruth; however, another fall in world tin prices at the end of 1985 cast yet another shadow over Cornwall's mines. The suspension of work at Geevor in April 1986, pushing the local unemployment figure to 40 per cent, sounded the alarm bells throughout mining communities whose immediate future now seemed bleak. China clay, on the other, has been spared from such sharply fluctuating fortunes and its late 19th-century expansion has been consolidated in the twentieth. The First World War was followed by a wave of mergers resulting in the near monopoly of English Clays Lovering Pochin (E.C.L.P.). By the mid-1980s annual profits had reached £75 million, most despatched from the ports of Par and Fowey, and the industry was firmly established as a principal employer in the central area of the county.

Agriculture and its ancillary trades has also consolidated its position as a dominant factor in the Cornish economy, although increasing mechanisation, particularly between the wars, drastically reduced the numbers employed in the industry. In the upland areas, sheep-rearing

112

became more widespread, while other farmers concentrated on meeting the nation's growing demand for dairy products. In the central and western parts of the county the mild climate has enabled the arable farms to grow two crops in the agricultural year, and since the late 19th century the usual combination has been early potatoes followed by the planting in August and September of either broccoli (winter cauliflower) or spring cabbage. Between 1890 and 1930 the proportion of broccoli being carried across the Tamar by rail increased tenfold to 32,000 tons a year.

*The* First and Last *public house, Land's End, as it looked in 1914*

The most striking economic development of the 20th century, and at the same time the most controversial, has been the advent of large-scale tourism. Hailed by many as a much-needed diversification, condemned by others as a despoiler of 'things Cornish', a commercial bogeyman which has reduced Cornwall to little more than 'the playground of England', the tourist industry has had a major effect on both the economic and social fabric of the county. The combination of a striking landscape and the element of mystery which stemmed from geographical remoteness attracted many intrepid 18th- and early 19th-century travellers; but Cornwall's connection to the national railway system in May 1859 opened the door to the up-country masses in search of their 'place in the sun'. Holiday promoters were hardly slow to grasp the opportunities which now unfolded and within six weeks the celebrated Thomas Cook had organised the first railway excursion across the Tamar. During the 1880s Cornwall became a fashionable haunt for the Victorian intelligentsia, and the output of the recently established artists' colonies at Newlyn and St Ives stimulated further interest. By the end of the century, with Penzance little more than seven hours away from London by rail, tourism had established itself as a vital counterbalance to the decay of Cornwall's traditional industries. Many coastal communities which had seemed doomed with the contraction of pilchard seining – Looe, Fowey, Mousehole and Perranporth are good examples – now earned a vital reprieve while Newquay, still a tiny fishing village in the 1850s, had grown into a community of 3,000 by 1901. Truro, with the attraction of its new cathedral and the enhanced status which came from its elevation to the rank of county town in 1889, also expanded as did its near neighbour, Falmouth, which emerged as a fashionable watering-hole for the more affluent. After the First World War the holiday trade grew steadily and then accelerated rapidly after the Second. By the late 1960s the County Planning Officer estimated that over 11 per cent of the working population were dependent on tourism, a proportion only exceeded by agriculture and the distributive trades. At the same time there were many who argued that the rise in the number of holiday homes to over 10,000 and the increasing influx of retired people were offsetting the economic advantages of this growth.

*Frontage of the Egyptian House, Penzance*

If the progressive expansion of the tourist trade has been responsible for the opening-up and increasing commercialisation of Cornwall, it has

113

*R. Morton Nance*

also contributed to a cultural reaction as enthusiasts have realised the importance of language, local traditions and history as bulwarks against the encroaching tide of trans-Atlantic uniformity. The Cornish language, extinct as a vernacular since the late 18th century and little more than an academic curiosity since, was dusted off and the grammar standardised, first by Henry Jenner who helped form the Celtic Cornish Society in 1901 and then by R. Morton Nance. Nance founded the Old Cornwall Society in 1920 with its purpose embodied in the motto 'Gather ye the fragments that are left that nothing be lost', and proceeded to produce a standard form of Unified Cornish. The Cornish Gorsedd was established in 1928, and four years later the Celtic Congress assembled in the county for the first time. The post-war years saw the production of a new dictionary, Cornish grammars and conversational booklets, and the language re-entered Cornish life in a mixed assortment of house names, boat names and rugby club mottoes.

The revival of things Cornish, which ran parallel with the re-emergence of political nationalism in Wales and Scotland, also led to the formation of Mebyon Kernow (Sons of Cornwall) in 1951. A successor to the *Tyr ha Tavas* movement of the late 1920s, MK pledged itself to maintain 'the character of Cornwall as a Celtic nation . . . and to promote the constitutional advance of Cornwall and its right to self-government in domestic affairs'. Initially the party was treated with considerable scepticism not only by outsiders but by most Cornish people themselves. Gradually, however, it has made a modest place for itself and, while it has been unable to make an impact in parliamentary elections, it has occasionally astounded the established national parties by winning local government contests, first in 1967 and more recently in May 1985 when MK candidate Colin Lawry unseated a Conservative county councillor in Penzance. Meanwhile, in 1972, the cultural renaissance received a major boost when the University of Exeter and Cornwall County Council combined to set up the Institute of Cornish Studies at Redruth with the aim of providing 'a focus for . . . all forms of research into Cornwall'. In 1969 one of the county's most celebrated adopted writers, Daphne du Maurier, published her rather pessimistically entitled book *Vanishing Cornwall*, but there are clearly many individuals and organisations determined to ensure that the identity of this special corner of the British Isles does not vanish altogether. Cornwall's present inhabitants, native-born and newcomers alike, might still manage a wry smile of satisfaction at the opinion of a Plymouth correspondent to the *Western Morning News* that 'we may have built the Tamar Bridge between us but there is still something pretty odd at the western end of it'.

*The Institute of Cornish Studies, Redruth*

114

# Bibliography

This bibliography is a guide to further reading rather than a complete list of references and source-material used in the writing of this book. I have excluded many 19th-century topographical works and parochial histories as most are inaccessible to the general reader as well as being of dubious reliability by today's standards. It has not been possible to cite individually the numerous specialist articles which I have used, but the enthusiast should particularly consult *Cornish Archaeology*, *Devon & Cornwall Notes and Queries*, *Old Cornwall*, the *Journal of the Royal Institution of Cornwall*, and the more recently established *Cornish Studies*.

Balchin, W. G. V., *Cornwall – History of the Landscape* (London, 1954)

Barnatt, J., *Prehistoric Cornwall* (Wellingborough, 1982)

Barton, D. B., *History of Tin Mining & Smelting in Cornwall* (Truro, 1967)

— *Essays in Cornish Mining History* (Truro, 1968)

— *A History of Copper Mining in Devon and Cornwall*, 3rd edn., (Truro, 1978)

Barton, R. M., *History of the Cornish China-Clay Industry* (Truro, 1966)

Boase, G. C. and Courtney, W., *Bibliotheca Cornubiensis* (3 vols., London, 1874–82)

Borlase, W., *Antiquities and Natural History of Cornwall* (2nd edn., London, 1769)

Bottrell, W., *Hearthside Stories of West Cornwall* (Penzance, 1870)

Brown, H. M., *The Church in Cornwall* (Truro, 1964)

Burl, A., *The Stone Circles of the British Isles* (London, 1976)

Coate, M., *Cornwall in the Great Civil War* (London, 1965)

Coleman, B. I., *The Church of England in the Mid-Nineteenth Century* (Historical Association, London, 1980)

Cunliffe, B., *Iron Age Communities in Britain* (London, 1974)

Davies, W., *Wales in the Early Middle Ages* (Leicester, 1982)

Denholm-Young, N., *Richard of Cornwall* (Oxford, 1947)

Ellis, P. B., *The Cornish Language and its Literature* (London, 1974)

Evans, J. G., *The Environment of Early Man in the British Isles* (London, 1975)

Finberg, H. P. R., *Tavistock Abbey* (Cambridge, 1951)

— *West-Country Historical Studies* (Newton Abbot, 1969)

Frere, S., *Britannia* (London, 1967)

Halliday, F. E. (ed.), *Carew's Survey of Cornwall, 1602* (London, 1969)

Hatcher, J., *Rural Economy and Society in the Duchy of Cornwall* (Cambridge, 1970)

Hencken, H., *The Archaeology of Cornwall and Scilly* (London, 1932)

Henderson, C., *Cornish Church Guide* (Truro, 1925)

— *Essays in Cornish History* (Oxford, 1935)

— *History of the Parish of Constantine* (Truro, 1937)

Hoskins, W. G., *The Westward Expansion of Wessex* (Leicester, 1960)

Hull, P. L. (ed.), *The Cartulary of St Michael's Mount* (Devon and Cornwall Record Society, n.s., v, 1962)

Jenkin, A. K. H., *Cornwall and its People* (Omnibus edn., Newton Abbot, 1983)

Laing, L., *Celtic Britain* (London, 1979)

Lewis, G. R., *The Stannaries* (2nd edn., Truro, 1965)

Noall, C., *Cornish Seines and Seiners* (Truro, 1972)

— *The Story of Cornwall's Lifeboats* (Truro, 1970)

Padel, O. J., *Cornish Place-Name Elements* (English Place-Name Society, vol. 56/57, Nottingham, 1985)

Pearce, J., *Wesleyism in Cornwall* (1964)

Pearce, S. M., *The Kingdom of Dumnonia* (Padstow, 1978)

— *The Archaeology of South-West Britain* (London, 1981)

Pevsner, N., *The Buildings of England — Cornwall* (London, 1951)

Pool, P. A. S., *History of the Town and Borough of Penzance* (Penzance, 1974)

— *The Death of Cornish* (Penzance, 1975)

— *A Cornish Farmer's Diary* (2nd edn., Penzance, 1978)

Rowe, J., *Cornwall in the Age of the Industrial Revolution* (Liverpool, 1953)

Rowse, A. L., *Tudor Cornwall* (London, 1941)

Sellers, I., *Nineteenth-Century Nonconformity* (London, 1977)

Sheppard, P., *The Historic Towns of Cornwall* (Truro, 1980)

Smith, A. S. D. and Hooper, E. G. R., *The Story of the Cornish Language* (Camborne, 1969)

Thomas, C., *Christian Antiquities of Camborne* (St Austell, 1967)

— *Christianity in Roman Britain to A.D. 500* (London, 1981)

— *Exploration of a Drowned Landscape, Archaeology and History of the Isles of Scilly* (London, 1985)

Thorn, C. and F. (eds.), *Domesday Book: Cornwall* (Chichester, 1979)

Wakelin, M., *Language and History in Cornwall* (Leicester, 1975)

Whetter, J., *Cornwall in the Seventeenth Century* (Padstow, 1978)

Witherick, M. E., *The medieval boroughs of Cornwall* (Southampton Research Series in Geography, 4 (1967), 41–60)

Woolf, C., *An Introduction to the Archaeology of Cornwall* (Truro, 1970)

# Index